Canadian Lynx

MACMILLAN McGRAW-HILL
Science

Lucy H. Daniel
Jay Hackett
Richard H. Moyer
JoAnne Vasquez

About the Cover

Canadian lynx live in forest areas. They are good climbers and can swim well in rivers and streams. They have padded feet that are like snowshoes. These help the lynx walk on top of the snow.

INQUIRY **What else would you like to know about Canadian lynx? Write your own question or questions to answer.**

McGraw Hill **Macmillan McGraw-Hill**

Program Authors

Dr. Lucy H. Daniel
Teacher, Consultant
Rutherford County Schools, North Carolina

Dr. Jay Hackett
Professor Emeritus of Earth Sciences
University of Northern Colorado

Dr. Richard H. Moyer
Professor of Science Education
University of Michigan-Dearborn

Dr. JoAnne Vasquez
Elementary Science Education Consultant
Mesa Public Schools, Arizona
NSTA Past President

Contributing Authors

Lucille Villegas Barrera, M.Ed.
Elementary Science Supervisor
Houston Independent School District
Houston, Texas

Mulugheta Teferi, M.A.
St. Louis Public Schools
St. Louis, Missouri

Dinah Zike, M.Ed.
Dinah Might Adventures LP
San Antonio, Texas

The features in this textbook entitled "Amazing Stories," as well as the unit openers, were developed in collaboration with the National Geographic Society's School Publishing Division.

Copyright © 2002 National Geographic Society. All rights reserved.

Students with print disabilities may be eligible to obtain an accessible, audio version of the pupil edition of this textbook. Please call Recording for the Blind & Dyslexic at 1-800-221-4792 for complete information.

The McGraw·Hill Companies

Macmillan McGraw-Hill

Published by Macmillan/McGraw-Hill, of McGraw-Hill Education, a division of The McGraw-Hill Companies, Inc., Two Penn Plaza, New York, New York 10121.

Printed in the United States of America
ISBN 0-02-281302-0/2

3 4 5 6 7 8 9 027/043 09 08 07 06 05

Life Science

Consultants

Dr. Carol Baskin
University of Kentucky
Lexington, KY

Dr. Joe W. Crim
University of Georgia
Athens, GA

Dr. Marie DiBerardino
Allegheny University of
Health Sciences
Philadelphia, PA

Dr. R. E. Duhrkopf
Baylor University
Waco, TX

Dr. Dennis L. Nelson
Montana State University
Bozeman, MT

Dr. Fred Sack
Ohio State University
Columbus, OH

Dr. Martin VanDyke
Denver, CO

Dr. E. Peter Volpe
Mercer University
Macon, GA

Earth Science

Consultants

Dr. Clarke Alexander
Skidaway Institute of
Oceanography
Savannah, GA

Dr. Suellen Cabe
Pembroke State University
Pembroke, NC

Dr. Thomas A. Davies
Texas A & M University
College Station, TX

Dr. Ed Geary
Geological Society of America
Boulder, CO

Dr. David C. Kopaska-Merkel
Geological Survey of Alabama
Tuscaloosa, AL

Physical Science

Consultants

Dr. Bonnie Buratti
Jet Propulsion Lab
Pasadena, CA

Dr. Shawn Carlson
Society of Amateur Scientists
San Diego, CA

Dr. Karen Kwitter
Williams College
Williamstown, MA

Dr. Steven Souza
Williamstown, MA

Dr. Joseph P. Straley
University of Kentucky
Lexington, KY

Dr. Thomas Troland
University of Kentucky
Lexington, KY

Dr. Josephine Davis Wallace
University of North Carolina
Charlotte, NC

Consultant for Primary Grades

Donna Harrell Lubcker
East Texas Baptist University
Marshall, TX

Teacher Reviewers (continued)

Beth Lewis
Wilmington, North Carolina

Cindy Hatchell
Wilmington, North Carolina

Cindy Kahler
Carrborro, North Carolina

Diane Leusky
Chapel Hill, North Carolina

Heather Sutton
Wilmington, North Carolina

Crystal Stephens
Valdese, North Carolina

Meg Millard
Chapel Hill, North Carolina

Patricia Underwood
Randleman, North Carolina

E. Joy Mermin
Chapel Hill, North Carolina

Yolanda Evans
Wilmington, North Carolina

Tim Gilbride
Pennsauken, New Jersey

Helene Reifowitz
Nesconsit, New York

Tina Craig
Tulsa, Oklahoma

Deborah Harwell
Lawton, Oklahoma

Kathleen Conn
West Chester, Pennsylvania

Heath Renninger Zerbe
Tremont, Pennsylvania

Patricia Armillei
Holland, Pennsylvania

Sue Workman
Cedar City, Utah

Peg Jensen
Hartford, Wisconsin

Letter from Sally Ride

When I was a girl I dreamed of being an astronaut. Learning about science made it happen!

I've always liked science. The planets and stars were my favorite. When I became an astronaut I began a great adventure! The space shuttle blasted off. Before I knew it, I was in space!

Maybe you have a dream like mine. Maybe you dream of exploring Mars. Or maybe your dream is something different. Whatever your dream is, science will help you. It will help you understand the world you live in.

Science launched me into space. It can take you places, too!

Reach for the stars!

Sally K. Ride

Be a Scientist! PAGE S1

v

UNIT A

Life Science

Plants and Animals PAGE A1

Homes for Plants and Animals PAGE B1

UNIT C

Earth Science

Changes on Earth PAGE C1

Earth Science

The Sun and Its Family PAGE D1

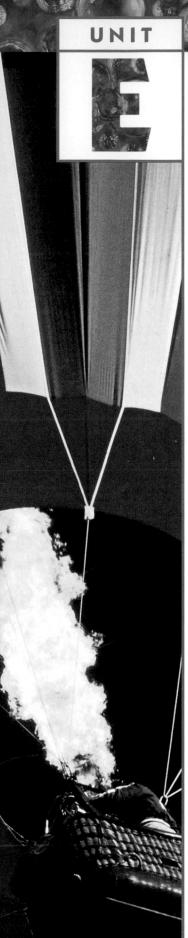

UNIT E

Physical Science

Matter and Energy PAGE E1

Physical Science

Watch It Move PAGE F1

Explore Activities

For Your Reference

Skills Handbook

Science Handbook

Health Handbook

Wash your hands after each activity.

Read all steps a few times before you start.

When you see this:

BE CAREFUL!

you should be careful.

Be careful with glass and sharp objects.

Cover your clothes or wear old ones.

Listen to the teacher.

Never taste or smell anything unless your teacher tells you to.

Keep your workplace neat. Clean up after you are done.

Tell the teacher about accidents and spills right away.

Wear goggles when you are told to.

Don't touch plants or animals unless your teacher tells you to.

Tell the teacher about spills and accidents right away.

Listen to the teacher.

Never taste or smell anything unless your teacher tells you to.

Stay with your group.

Never throw your trash on the ground.

Put living things back where you found them.

Be a Scientist!

What is this?

A flower!

Have you ever wondered
about the things you see?
How do you find out about
the world around you?

Scientists use skills to answer questions about the world. Here are some skills they use.

- observe
- infer
- predict
- communicate
- measure
- put things in order
- compare
- classify
- investigate
- make models
- draw conclusions

Scientists **observe**.
Can you find something
hiding on the leaves?

Scientists **infer**.
At what time of year
was this picture taken?

Scientists **predict**.
What do you think will happen when the weather gets colder?

Scientists **communicate**.
Share your answer with others.

poppy

pansy

daisy

Scientists **measure**.
Which flower is the smallest?
Which one is the largest?

sunflower

Scientists **put things in order**. Put the flowers in order from smallest to largest.

Scientists **compare**.
How are the flowers alike?
How are they different?

gladiolus

daffodil

iris

Classify

Scientists **classify**.
Put the flowers into
groups that are alike.

orchid

lilac

Scientists **investigate**.
What do flowers need to grow?
How could you find out?

Scientists **make models**.
How can a model help you learn
about plants?

Scientists **draw conclusions**.
What parts do most plants have?

Scientists use skills to learn what is known about the world. Here are some skills they use.

- **read**
- **use pictures**
- **write**
- **find information**
- **use tools**

Amazing Plants

Venus's fly trap

This plant is special!
It traps and eats insects!

An insect touches the hairs on this plant's leaves.

The leaves snap shut. The insect gets trapped inside.

The plant eats the insect. All that is left is the insect's hard body covering.

Scientists **read** and **use pictures**.
Can a plant eat an insect?
How do you know?

Scientists **write**.
Look at the picture.
Write about it.

Scientists **find information.**
Use the Internet or a book to
find out about desert plants.

scissors

mirror

hand lens

thermometer

ruler

Scientists **use tools**.
Who is a scientist?
Pick the right tool to find out.

Who
is a
scientist?
You are!

UNIT A

Exploring Indiana

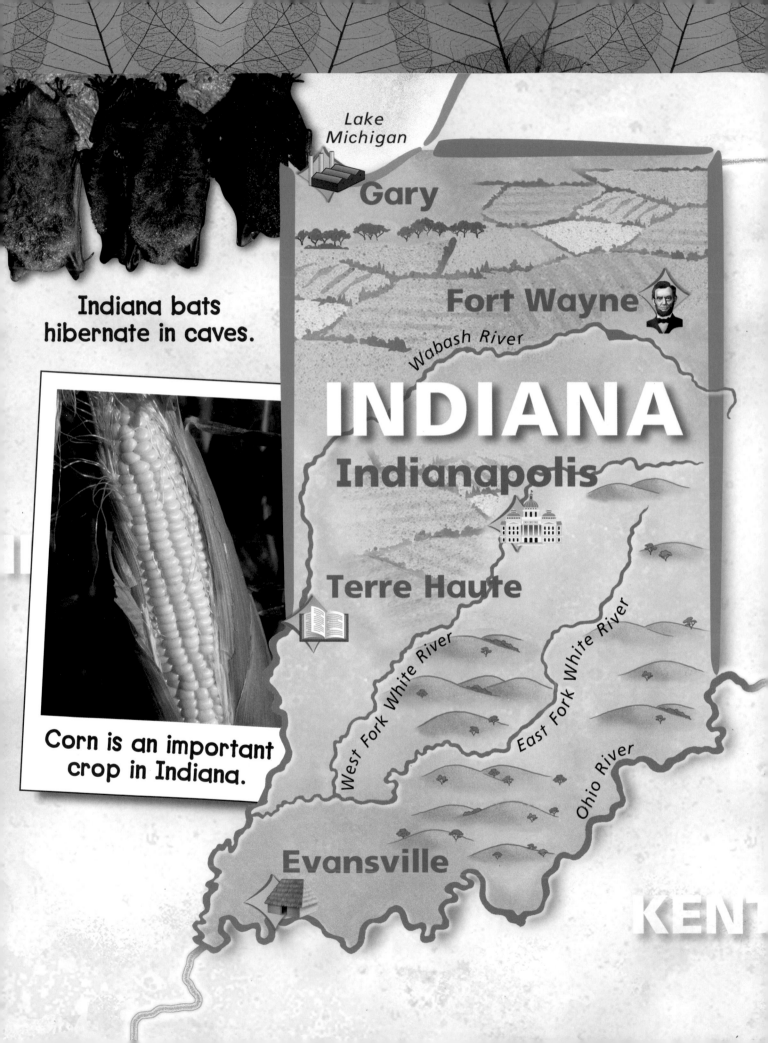

Indiana bats
hibernate in caves.

Corn is an important
crop in Indiana.

Lake
Michigan

Gary

Fort Wayne

Wabash River

INDIANA

Indianapolis

Terre Haute

West Fork White River

East Fork White River

Ohio River

Evansville

KEN

Exploring Indiana

The Karner blue butterfly is endangered.

The Indiana State Fair is great fun.

From Seed to Seed

Plants drop seeds on the ground.
A new plant can grow from a seed.
What do plants need to grow?

Corn kernels are seeds
that can grow.

Leaves and roots
grow from a seed.

Some roots help a
corn plant stand tall.

Look at the pictures of corn growing. The seeds, or kernels, fall to the ground. New corn plants can grow from the kernels.

You can see corn flowers at the top of the plants.

This ear of corn can be food for people or animals.

How Animals Stay Safe

Animals need many things. Animals need food, water, air, and space. Animals also need to live in a safe place.

Bittern

Indiana bats

Birds make nests to hold their eggs. Birds keep their eggs warm. Soon the baby birds hatch. The adult birds bring food to the babies in the nest.

Some animals have colors that make them hard to see.

White-tailed deer

Karner blue butterfly

ACTIVITY

- Pick three animals.

- List ways these animals stay safe.

- How does each animal find food, water, air, and space?

Indiana Test Prep

1 Animals need air, water, and

   A clothes.

   B friends.

   C food.

   D sunlight.

2 Baby birds get food from

   A adult birds.

   B the Sun.

   C cats.

   D water.

deer   bittern   bat

Use the pictures for questions 3–4.

3 Which two animals can fly?

4 Which animal keeps safe by running fast?

Life Science

UNIT A

Plants and Animals

LOOK!

Pandas like to eat bamboo, a treelike plant. What else do pandas like to do? Take a good look!

Plants and Animals

minerals, A7

flower, A12

fruit, A13

seeds, A13

pollen, A16

life cycle, A18

oxygen, A23

Did You Ever Wonder?

Where do blueberries come from? They grow on bushes found in the wild and on blueberry farms. Do you know other plants that grow fruit?

INQUIRY SKILL **Compare** two fruits. What do they look like? How do they grow? How do people use them?

Plants Are Living Things

Get Ready

Can you find things in this picture that are living? Can you find things that are not living? Tell how things in this picture are alike and different.

Inquiry Skill

You **classify** when you put things into groups to show how they are alike.

Explore Activity

Which of these are living?

What to do

1. **Classify** things in your classroom. Find three or more living things. Find three or more nonliving things.

2. Record the things in a chart.

3. FURTHER INQUIRY Share your chart with a partner. Tell how you knew how to **classify** each thing.

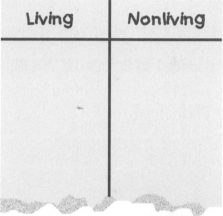

Living	Nonliving

Are plants living things?

Living things are found in many places. There are different kinds in different places. Like all living things, plants grow and change. To grow, plants need food, water, air, and space. Plants can make other living things like themselves. Nonliving things can not do this.

▷ **How can you tell these plants are living things?**

pine tree

tiger lilies

How are plants alike?

Plants need light, water, and air. They use these things to make food. They also need **minerals**. Minerals come from tiny bits of rock and soil. Plants use minerals to stay healthy.

▷ **How are all of these plants alike?**

green beans

How are plants different?

Plants may have different shapes, sizes, and colors. Plants may be as small as a penny or as tall as a house. Many plants have green leaves. Some plants have colorful flowers.

Many plants grow straight up from the ground. Other plants, such as vines, grow up walls or along the ground.

wisteria vine

peach tree

Trees are plants. They have hard trunks. Some trees, such as peach trees, grow fruit that we can eat.

Some plants, such as evergreens, stay green all year. They can grow tall like trees or stay short like shrubs.

lily of the valley

evergreen shrub

 **How are these plants different from each other?**

Think and Write

1. How are plants like all living things?

2. How are all plants alike?

3. Name two ways that plants can be different from one another.

 LOG ON Visit **www.science.mmhschool.com** for more information about plants.

Parts of Plants

Get Ready

Why do you think this plant is leaning toward the window? Predict what might happen if the plant was not near a window.

Inquiry Skill

You **predict** when you use what you know to tell what will happen.

Explore Activity

What do leaves need?

What you need

two potted plants

foil

What to do

1 Put the plants in a sunny place. Cover the leaves of Plant B with foil. Keep the soil moist.

2 **Predict** what will happen to each plant.

3 Record what you observe each day for a week.

4 Were your predictions correct? What do leaves need?

5 **FURTHER INQUIRY**

Predict what will happen when you remove the foil. Then observe what happens.

What happened?

Day	Plant A	Plant B
Day 1		
Day 2		
Day 3		
Day 4		

What do plant parts do?

The parts of a plant help the plant get what it needs. Some parts help it get light, water, air, and minerals. Other parts help it make new plants.

leaves
Leaves take in air and use light to make food.

flowers
Flowers make seeds.

stem
A stem holds up the plant. It carries food and water to all the plant parts.

roots
Roots hold the plant in the soil. They take in water and minerals from the soil.

fruit
The **fruit** is the part of a plant that grows around seeds. It protects the seeds.

seeds
Seeds can grow into new plants.

Think and Write

1. Name the parts of a plant.

2. How do roots help a plant get what it needs?

? **How does each plant part help the plant?**

MORE TO READ Read **Plants and Flowers** by Sally Hewitt.

Plants Make New Plants

Get Ready

Think about cutting open a big, orange pumpkin. What do you think you would find inside it? What plant part do you think a pumpkin is?

Inquiry Skill

You **infer** when you use what you know to figure something out.

Explore Activity

What is inside an apple?

whole apple

What to do

1 Look at a whole apple. Predict what is inside.

half an apple

2 Look at half an apple. Use a hand lens. How many seeds do you see?

3 Draw what you see.

hand lens

4 FURTHER INQUIRY Infer how fruits protect seeds.

paper

crayons

How do plants make seeds?

Different plants have different ways to make seeds. Many plants grow flowers. Inside a flower is a powder called **pollen**. Pollen is needed to make seeds.

When an insect lands on a flower, pollen may stick to the insect. Then it carries the pollen from flower to flower.

pepper plant

Pollen helps make seeds grow inside the flower.

flower

As the seeds grow, the flower changes. The outside parts of the flower fall off. Fruit grows around the seeds to protect them.

fruit

seeds

When the fruit is full-grown, it may fall off the plant. Some seeds may grow into new plants if they are planted in soil.

How do seeds grow into new plants?

A **life cycle** shows how a living thing grows, lives, and dies. A plant's life cycle starts with a seed. The outside of the seed is covered by a seed coat. When a seed gets water, warmth, and air, it can begin to grow.

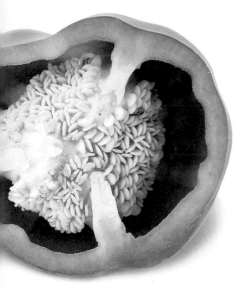

First, a small root grows down. The stem grows up. When a stem breaks through the soil, it is called a sprout.

seeds

sprout

seedling

Soon the sprout grows leaves and can make its own food. It is now called a seedling.

adult pepper plant

In time, the plant will grow to look like the plant it came from. It will make seeds, and the life cycle will begin again.

▶ **How does a seed grow into a plant?**

Think and Write

1. What is pollen?

2. How do insects help plants to grow seeds?

3. What is a life cycle?

MORE TO READ Read **From Seed to Plant** by Gail Gibbons.

Everyone Needs Plants

Get Ready

Have you ever wondered what the world would be like without plants? Look carefully at this picture. What things come from plants?

Inquiry Skill

You **infer** when you use what you know to figure something out.

Explore Activity

What are made from plants?

What to do

1 Go on a plant hunt in your classroom.

2 **Infer** which objects are made from plants. Look for other objects that are not made from plants.

3 Fill in a chart like this one.

Made from Plants	Not Made from Plants

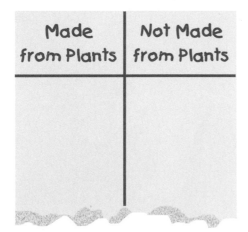

4 **FURTHER INQUIRY**
Infer why plants are important to us. Talk about it with a partner.

How do people use plants?

Many things you use every day come from plants. The cotton plant can be used to make clothes.

Some plants are used to make medicine. One plant used for medicine is aloe. The leaves of the aloe plant contain oil. This oil helps heal minor burns and scrapes.

cotton

aloe

lumber

paper

furniture

pine
tree

Trees are used for wood and for paper products. People use wood to build houses, furniture, and many other things.

Most importantly, plants make **oxygen**. People, animals, and plants need oxygen to live. As plants make food for themselves, they give off oxygen into the air.

▶ **What are some ways people use plants?**

How do people use plants for food?

People eat different plant parts. Apples are fruits. Carrots are roots. We eat leaves, such as lettuce, and flowers, such as cauliflower. The seeds of certain grasses are grains. Grains are made into flour, cereal, and bread.

Some seeds and fruits have oils that are used for cooking. For example, peanuts and corn are plants used to make oil.

corn

corn oil

corn muffin

margarine

Herbs and spices are parts of plants used to flavor foods. Some herbs are mint and parsley. Some spices you may use are pepper and cinnamon.

mint

cinnamon

▶ **Where do the foods in these pictures come from?**

cornflakes

Think and Write

1. What kinds of things do we get from plants?

2. What is the most important thing we get from plants? Tell why.

3. What are some foods we get from plants?

HOME ACTIVITY Look around your home. What do you see that is made from wood or paper?

corn tortillas

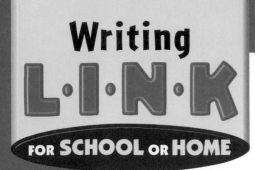

Pretty and Harmful

The water hyacinth is from South America. People planted it in Florida because it is pretty, but it is harmful. This plant grows very fast. It stops other plants from growing.

Try This!

Writing a Poem Discover other plants that cause big changes in the land and water. Write a poem about how they are harmful.

Plan a Plant Menu

We need to eat food to get energy. Think about what you ate today. Did you eat any plants or food made from plants?

The Special of the day is Plants.

Try This!

Plan a meal that uses only plants and things that are made from plants. Write a menu and draw what the meal might look like.

Chapter 1 Review

Vocabulary

flower, A12

fruit, A13

life cycle, A18

minerals, A7

oxygen, A23

pollen, A16

seeds, A13

Use each word once for items 1–7.

1 A ____ shows how a living thing grows, lives, and dies.

2 Some plants grow from ____ .

3 Plants give off ____ into the air.

4 Plants take in ____ from rocks and soil.

5 The powder made by flowers is called ____ .

6 The plant part that makes seeds is called a ____ .

7 The plant part that grows around a seed and protects it is a ____ .

Science Ideas

8 What do all plants need to stay alive?

9 What parts of this plant are not shown in the picture?

READ
Mr. Hobson's Garden by Marc Gave

Did You Ever Wonder?

INQUIRY SKILL **Observe** parts of different plants. You can go to the market or a garden. How are the leaves alike and different? What do the flowers look like?

2 Animals

mammals, A34

reptiles, A34

amphibian, A35

predator, A40

prey, A40

food chain, A41

shelter, A42

larva, A48

pupa, A48

Did You Ever Wonder?

Do animals take care of their young? Some do! The manatee teaches its calf how to swim and find food. What will this manatee calf look like as an adult?

INQUIRY SKILL **Compare** a young animal and its mother. Tell how they are alike and different. Tell how the young animal will grow.

All Kinds of Animals

Get Ready

There are many kinds of animals. Look at these animals. How are they alike? How are they different?

Inquiry Skill

You **classify** when you put things into groups to show how they are alike.

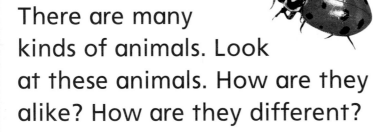

Explore Activity

How can we classify animals?

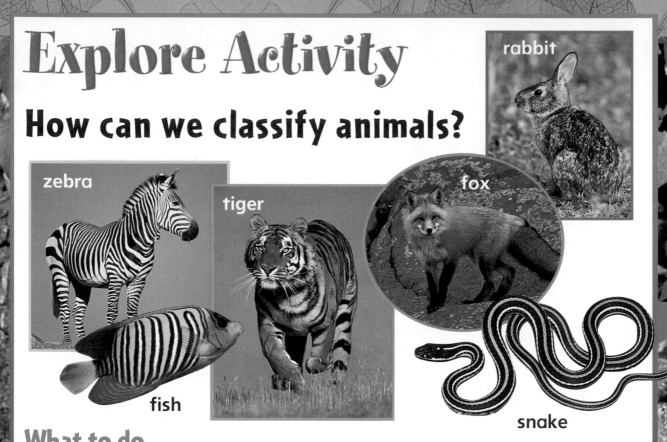

zebra

rabbit

tiger

fox

fish

snake

What to do

1 Compare the animals in these pictures.

2 Make a Venn diagram like this one. **Classify** the animals.

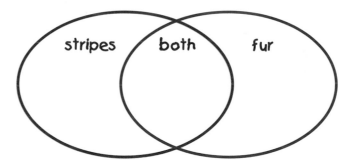

stripes   both   fur

3 Write the names of the animals in the correct parts of the circles. Tell how you decided where each animal belongs.

4 FURTHER INQUIRY Think of more animals that you could **classify**. Write them in your diagram.

beetle

What are some animal groups?

Scientists classify animals into groups. To do this, they look at ways animals are the same as or different from other animals.

insects
Insects have three body parts and six legs. They have hard body coverings. Their young hatch from eggs.

rattlesnake

reptiles
Reptiles have scaly skin. Most reptiles lay eggs.

mammals
Female mammals make milk for their babies. Mammals have hair or fur. They breathe with body parts called lungs.

lion

amphibians

Almost all **amphibians** begin their lives in water. They often have smooth, moist skin that helps them to live both in water and on land.

tree frog

goldfinch

birds

Birds are the only animals with feathers. Birds have two wings and two legs. They also have beaks and lay eggs.

> **How are fish different from the other animal groups?**

butterfly fish

Think and Write

1. What are six groups of animals?

2. How are mammals and birds different from one another?

fish

Fish live in water. They breathe with body parts called gills. Fish have fins to move through the water.

LOG ON Visit **www.science.mmhschool.com** to learn more about animals.

Animals Meet Their Needs

Get Ready

Look at this fish. What is it doing? Tell how the fish is getting what it needs to live.

Inquiry Skill

You **communicate** when you share your ideas with others.

Explore Activity

paper rolls

Why are eyes where they are?

What to do

1 Stand with your back to a partner. Look through the tubes.

2 Your partner will move his or her arms forward. Tell when you first see their fingers.

3 Now try without the tubes. **Communicate** what happened. Compare what you see with and without the tubes.

4 FURTHER INQUIRY

Communicate why fish might have eyes on the side of their heads.

What do animals need?

Animals need air, water, food, and space. Big animals need a lot of these things. Smaller animals need less. All animals need a safe place to live and have their young.

Different kinds of animals live in different places. Some live on land. Some live in the water. But each animal can get what it needs in the place where it lives.

 What do these birds need to live?

herons

How do animals get water and air?

Animals need water. Some drink from lakes and streams. Other animals get water from the food they eat. You need water, too.

All animals need oxygen. Some animals get oxygen from the air. Fish get oxygen from the water. They use gills to breathe. Sea mammals have lungs. They must come to the surface of the water for air.

▶ **How do these animals get what they need?**

humpback whale

lions

How do animals get food?

Animals use their senses and body parts to get the food they need. Some eat only plants. Some eat only other animals. Some eat both plants and animals.

An animal that hunts another animal for food is called a **predator**. An animal that is being hunted is called **prey**.

Sharks use their senses of smell and hearing to hunt their prey. Their strong tails help them swim fast.

▶ **What do these animals use to get food?**

Raccoons can use their front paws to search for food.

Rabbits have strong, flat front teeth. They help rabbits eat plants.

What is a food chain?

All living things need food. Food gives them energy. A **food chain** shows how one living thing gets energy from another living thing. The Sun, a plant, a caterpillar, a bird, and a cat make up one food chain.

The plant uses sunlight to make its own food.

A caterpillar eats the green leaves.

A bird eats the caterpillar

A cat eats the bird.

▷ **What does the bird in this food chain eat?**

How do animals stay safe?

Animals stay safe in many ways. Many use their senses to keep on the alert. Some find **shelter**, or places they can live in and be safe. A mouse can find shelter in a hole. Other animals, like gazelles, can run very fast. Their great speed helps them escape from predators.

gazelles

mouse

Some animals' bodies help them stay safe. A turtle has a hard shell. When danger is near, it can pull its body inside the shell to keep safe.

This insect blends in with the leaves around it. This helps the insect hide from birds and other predators.

katydid

? What are these animals doing to stay safe?

box turtle

Think and Write

1. What are the needs of animals?

2. What is a food chain?

3. What are two ways that animals stay safe?

 **MORE TO READ** Read **Amazing Animals** by Robin Bernard.

Animals Grow and Change

Get Ready

Look at the young swans. How do you think they will look in one year? Why do you think so?

Inquiry Skill

You put things **in order** when you tell what happens first, next, and last.

Explore Activity

How do animals grow and change?

What you need

paper

crayons

What to do

1 Draw a baby animal. Next, draw the animal when it is a little older. Then draw it as an adult.

2 Mix up the pictures. Trade pictures with a partner.

3 Put your partner's pictures **in order**. Tell which one comes first, next, and last. How does the animal grow and change?

4 **FURTHER INQUIRY**

Draw a seed, sprout, and an adult plant. Have a partner put the pictures **in order**. How does the plant change?

How does a black bear grow and change?

All animals grow and change until they die. They grow to look like their parents.

eight months old
The cub begins to climb and play. This helps it build muscles. It has most of its teeth, but still needs its parents to find food.

three months old
At birth a black bear cub is blind. It is tiny and has no fur. It grows fast. After three months it weighs about ten pounds. It does not have all of its teeth yet. It gets milk from its mother.

A cub stays with its mother for about one year. Then, it is nearly full-grown. It can find food on its own. Soon, the young bear leaves its mother.

> ▶ **How is a black bear at three months old different from an adult bear?**

adult
An adult black bear can grow as tall as six feet. It can have its own young. The adult keeps growing and changing until it dies.

How does a butterfly grow and change?

All insects need food, air, and space to grow. Butterflies begin life looking very different from their parents. They go through four stages as they grow into adults.

pupa
The caterpillar forms a hard case around itself. This is the **pupa** stage. Inside the case the pupa changes into a butterfly.

larva
When the egg hatches, a caterpillar crawls out. This is the **larva** stage. The plant is food for the caterpillar. It eats until it is ready for the next stage. Then it attaches itself to a leaf or branch.

egg
A butterfly starts its life as an egg. Most butterflies lay their eggs on plants.

adult

Soon the butterfly comes out of the case. Now the butterfly is an adult. It looks like other adult butterflies of its kind. It can lay eggs. Then it grows older and dies.

? **What happens when the insect is in the pupa stage?**

Think and Write

1. How does a black bear change during its life?

2. What are the four stages of a butterfly's life cycle?

3. How is a black bear's life cycle different from a butterfly's life cycle?

HOME ACTIVITY Make four pictures, each of which shows a stage of your life.

ALL
ABOUT EGGS

written by
DEBBY SLIER

illustrated by
KA BOTZIS

Eggs-ellent Cards!

Different animals lay their eggs in different places. To find out where, read *All About Eggs* by Debby Slier.

Try This!

Make an egg-shaped card. Pick an animal that lays eggs. Where does that animal lay eggs? Draw a picture of the egg on the front. On the inside, draw what the animal looks like when it is born.

Science Newsroom CD-ROM
Choose **Classifying** to learn how to group things.

Swim Stars!

Penguins, sea turtles, and sea lions swim in the ocean. Which animal swims the fastest? Read the graph to find out.

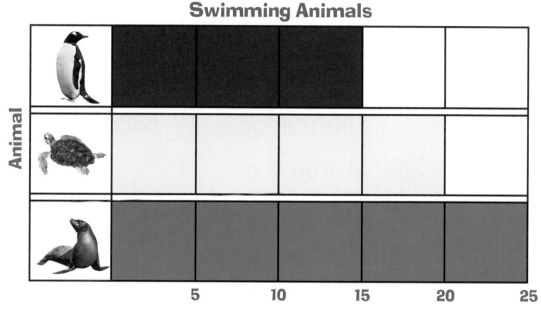

Swimming Animals

Animal

5   10   15   20   25

Miles per hour

Try This!

1. List the swimmers from fastest to slowest.

2. How many miles per hour can the fastest animal swim?

3. How many miles per hour can the slowest animal swim?

Chapter 2 Review

Vocabulary

amphibian, A35

food chain, A41

larva, A48

mammals, A34

predator, A40

prey, A40

pupa, A48

reptiles, A34

shelter, A42

Use each word once for items 1–9.

1 The Sun, a leaf, a worm, a bird, and a cat together are an example of a _____ .

2 An animal that hunts other animals for food is a _____ .

3 An animal that is hunted by another animal is called _____ .

4 A frog is an _____ .

5 An animal can keep safe in a _____ .

6 All _____ have hair or fur on their bodies.

7 Animals that have scaly skin are called _____ .

8 Another word for a caterpillar is _____ .

9 When a caterpillar makes a hard case, it is called a _____ .

Science Ideas

10 How do you know this animal is a mammal?

Inquiry Skill: Put Things in Order

11 Put the life cycle of this butterfly in order.

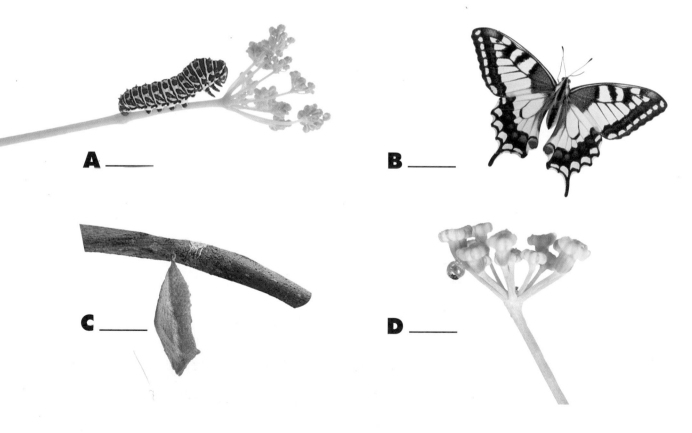

A _____

B _____

C _____

D _____

Did You Ever Wonder? [INQUIRY SKILL] Choose an insect. **Make a model** of its life cycle.

Monkey Business!

Have you ever needed a helping hand? A place called Helping Hands in Boston, Massachusetts, teaches monkeys to help people with disabilities.

Monkey helpers can turn on lights, open doors, fetch water bottles . . .

First, a monkey stays with a family for about six years. It learns how to be around people.

Next, the monkey stays with a trainer. The monkey learns how to do jobs. Sample jobs are picking up dropped things, dialing a phone, and loading a computer disk. After a year and a half, the monkey is matched with a disabled person.

... load a tape into a VCR ...

... and even scratch itches.

What would it be like to have a monkey helper? Write a story about it.

LOG ON Visit **www.science.mmhschool.com** to find out more about animal helpers.

Plant Mobile

Look through magazines for plant pictures. Cut out one of each:

- an object made from plants
- a food made from plants
- a fruit or seed

Animal Family

People and animals in the same family can look like each other. Look at the kittens with their mother. How are the kittens alike? How are they different? Write or tell what you observe.

UNIT B

Exploring Indiana

Yellow tiger
swallowtail

What are some animals that live in cities?

Exploring Indiana

Forest Animals

Opossum

When is the last time you visited a forest?

Many animals live in the forest. You might see opossums, snakes, and salamanders in the forest.

Rattlesnake

Copperhead

Moles, bobcats, and frogs may also be found in Indiana forests. Look and listen for birds when you walk through a forest.

Spring peeper

Bobcat

Tiger salamander

Star-nosed mole

Animals of Lake Michigan

Lake Michigan is one of the largest lakes in the world. In some places, the lake is more than 900 feet deep. Many different kinds of fish live in Lake Michigan.

Chinook Salmon

Dunes and Lake Michigan

Lampreys can grow to be two feet long. They have sucker-disks with sharp teeth. They attach this sucker-disk to a fish then feed on it.

Zebra mussels have two shells. In some places, there are so many zebra mussels, they cover docks and clog pipes.

ACTIVITY

Draw some things you would see in Lake Michigan. Make a bulletin board display of your drawings.

1 Which of these animals does not live in a forest?

   A salamander

   B trout

   C bobcat

   D chipmunk

2 Which of these animals live in Lake Michigan?

   A rattlesnake

   B spring peeper

   C bobcat

   D zebra mussel

Life Science

UNIT
B

Homes for Plants
and Animals

LOOK!

What is this animal?
Where does it live?
Take a good look!

Homes for Plants and Animals

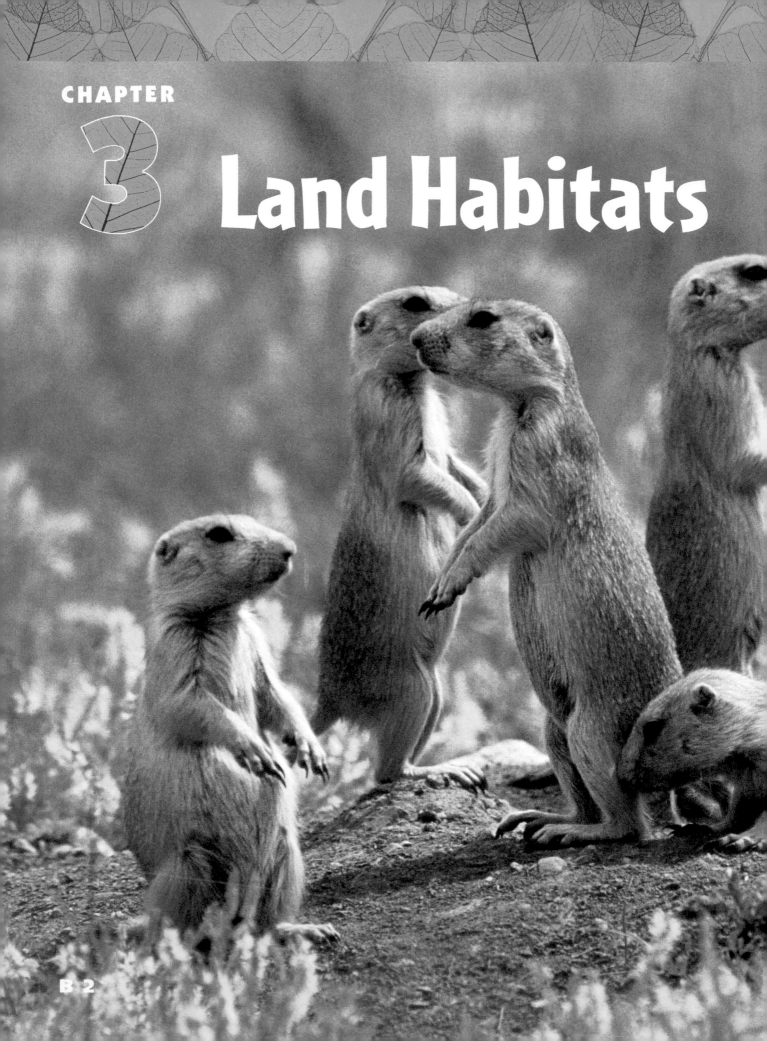

3 Land Habitats

Vocabulary

habitat, B6
woodland
 forest, B10
migrate, B13
rain forest, B16
desert, B20
Arctic, B24

Did You Ever Wonder?

Why do prairie dogs pop up out of holes? They live below the ground. When a prairie dog sees danger, it barks and hides in the ground.

INQUIRY SKILL Communicate how a cat acts when it sees danger. Tell how you know.

Where Plants and Animals Live

Get Ready

Living in the mountains is not easy! The weather is cold. The ground is rocky. How does this mountain goat get what it needs to live?

Inquiry Skill

You **communicate** when you talk, write, or draw to share your ideas.

Explore Activity

Where do animals live?

What to do

1 Look at the footprints. What animal do you think made them?

2 How does the shape of the feet help this animal? **Communicate** your idea with a partner.

3 Draw a picture of the animal. Show where it lives.

4 FURTHER INQUIRY **Communicate** what it needs to live. How does it get food and water?

What is a habitat?

A **habitat** is a place where plants and animals meet their needs. Different plants and animals live in different habitats.

The animals in these pictures live near water. This is where they can find what they need to live.

water strider

otter

The animals in a habitat need plants. They also need each other. Some animals use plants for shelter. Many eat plants. Some animals eat other animals. This bird lives near water because it eats the fish that live there.

? How is the kingfisher meeting its needs?

kingfisher

Think and Write

1. What is a habitat?

2. What do animals get from their habitats?

 **HOME ACTIVITY** Take a walk with a family member. Look for plants and animals in a habitat.

catfish

Life in a Woodland Forest

Get Ready

A place with many trees is a good habitat for a chipmunk. How could you show where a chipmunk lives?

Inquiry Skill

You **make a model** when you make something to show a place or a thing.

Explore Activity

What is a forest like?

What to do

1 **Make a model** of a forest. Place the soil, plant, and rocks in a bottle.

2 Water the soil. Add the pill bug. Cover the bottle with plastic wrap. Poke holes in it. Place it near a window.

3 Observe your model. Record how it changes.

4 **FURTHER INQUIRY** **Make a model** of the forest in winter. Draw a picture to show how it would change.

bottle

soil

plant

PLASTIC WRAP

plastic wrap

rocks

plastic spoon

pill bug

What lives in a woodland forest?

A **woodland forest** is a habitat that gets enough rain and sunlight for trees to grow well. Some animals may use the trees for food. Some eat nuts and insects found on trees.

mushrooms

raccoon

A tree can be a home for many living things. Plants may grow on the outside of the tree. Small animals may make their homes inside the tree.

Some animals may use other animals for shelter. A small insect may live on a bigger animal's body.

woodpecker

▷ **What are some animals that live in this woodland forest?**

insect living on a deer

foxes

How does a woodland forest change?

A woodland forest has four seasons. In spring many forest animals have their young. Leaves begin to grow on trees.

spring

deer

In summer woodland forests are warm. Leaves on the trees are green. Animals can find a lot of food to eat.

deer mouse

summer

In fall the weather gets cool. The leaves on many trees change color and fall to the ground. Sometimes plant seeds stick to animals. Animals move them to new places where they may grow.

Some forest animals store food for the winter. Many birds **migrate**, or move to warmer places.

In winter many trees have no leaves. It is cold and food is harder to find. Some animals go into a deep sleep.

fall

bison

chipmunk

winter

 How do the trees in a woodland forest change during fall and winter?

Think and Write

1. What is a woodland forest?

2. How do animals help the plants of a woodland forest?

Make a book of seasons. Draw a picture of what you do in each season.

Life in a Rain Forest

Get Ready

These fuzzy creatures are leaf bats. They live in a habitat called a rain forest. How are they using the leaf to meet their needs?

Inquiry Skill

You **infer** when you use what you know to figure something out.

Explore Activity

How can a rain forest animal find shelter?

What to do

1 Fold a paper plate in half. Glue five cotton balls inside the fold.

2 Stand up the plate like a tent. Put it in the tray. Pour a little water over the paper plate.

3 Observe the cotton balls.

4 **FURTHER INQUIRY** **Infer** why leaf bats find shelter inside rain forest leaves.

paper plate

cotton balls

glue

aluminum tray

water

What lives in a rain forest?

A **rain forest** is a habitat where it rains almost every day. It is warm in many rain forests. There can be more than 70 inches of rain each year. Because there is a lot of rain, many trees and plants grow well. The trees and plants are food and shelter for many animals.

A tree frog finds water.

An ocelot hunts for food.

There are many tall trees in a rain forest. The tops of the trees get a lot of sunlight. Less sunlight reaches the rain forest floor.

Monkeys and parrots are two kinds of animals that live in the tops of trees. They eat the leaves, fruits, and nuts that grow there.

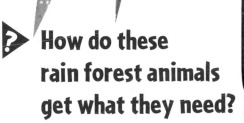
parrot

monkey

? **How do these rain forest animals get what they need?**

Think and Write

1. Describe a rain forest.

2. How do some rain forest animals use plants?

MORE TO READ

Read **Nature's Green Umbrella: Tropical Rain Forests** by Gail Gibbons.

Life in a Desert

Get Ready

This habitat is hot and dry. It gets less than ten inches of rain a year. How do you think this plant can live with very little rainfall?

Inquiry Skill

You **draw a conclusion** when you use what you observe to explain something.

Explore Activity

How does the shape of a leaf help a plant?

What you need

paper towels

scissors

water

PLASTIC WRAP

plastic wrap

What to do

1 Cut two leaf shapes from the paper towels. Roll up one leaf.

 **BE CAREFUL!** Scissors are sharp!

2 Place both leaf shapes on plastic wrap. Wet them both.

3 Check both leaf shapes every 15 minutes. Which leaf shape stayed wet longer?

4 FURTHER INQUIRY
Draw a **conclusion** about which kind of leaf you might find in a dry place.

What lives in a desert?

A **desert** is a dry habitat. It gets less rain in a year than most plants and animals need to live.

Some desert plants, such as a cactus, can live a long time without rain. They store water in their thick stems.

Some desert animals get the water they need from their food.

jackrabbit

cactus

rattlesnake

lizard

Some deserts are very hot during the day. Many animals hide below ground or under rocks to keep cool. At night they come out to look for food.

 What are some animals that live in the desert?

Think and Write

1. What is a desert?

2. How do some desert animals keep cool when the sun is hot?

 LOG ON Visit **www.science.mmhschool.com** to learn more about deserts.

Life in the Arctic

Arctic fox in summer

Get Ready

This Arctic fox had a dark coat last summer. Then its coat turned white in winter. What color coat do you think the fox will have next summer? Tell why.

Inquiry Skill

You **predict** when you use what you know to tell what you think will happen.

Arctic fox in winter

Explore Activity

How can color help animals hide?

white paper

20 white circles

20 brown circles

What to do

1 Fold the white paper. Spread out the circles on one half of the paper. Fold over the other side.

2 Your partner will uncover the circles and count to ten. Pick up as many circles as you can.

3 How many circles of each color did you pick up? How does color make it easier or harder to pick up the circles?

4 FURTHER INQUIRY
Predict what will happen if you use brown paper. Then try it.

What lives in the Arctic?

The **Arctic** is a very cold place near the North Pole. Snow is on the ground for much of the year. It melts for only a short time in the summer.

In summer plants can grow. They grow very low to the ground. This helps them stay safe from strong winds. Many animals eat these plants.

Arctic plants

musk ox

caribou

Arctic terns

In winter most plants die. Animals that eat plants migrate, or move, to warmer places to find food.

Some animals have white winter coats to blend in with the snow. This helps keep them safe. Polar bears make snow dens. Safe in the dens, the female bears can give birth to their cubs.

▷ **How do these living things meet their needs?**

polar bears

Think and Write

1. When do most plants grow in the Arctic?

2. Why do some animals leave the Arctic in the winter?

MORE TO READ Read **Crinkleroot's Guide to Knowing Animal Habitats** by Jim Arnosky.

What is your habitat like?

You have learned about different habitats. You live in a habitat, too. Observe the plants and animals that live near you.

Try This!

Writing that Compares Look at these pictures. Compare the habitat where you live with one of these habitats. Write how the habitats are alike. Then write how they are different.

In the Rain Forest

It rains almost every day in the rain forest. The raindrops in the graph show how many inches of rain fall in April, May, and June.

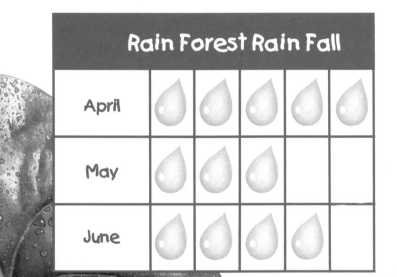

Rain Forest Rain Fall

April	💧	💧	💧	💧	💧
May	💧	💧	💧		
June	💧	💧	💧	💧	

Try This!

Use the graph. Compare the amounts of rainfall. Did more rain fall during May or June? Tell how you know.

Chapter 3 Review

Vocabulary

Arctic, B24

desert, B20

habitat, B6

migrate, B13

rain forest, B16

woodland forest, B10

Use each word once for items 1–6.

1 A place where plants and animals find what they need to live is a _____ .

2 A habitat where very little rain falls is called a _____ .

3 Animals _____ when they move to warmer places in winter.

4 A habitat where many trees grow and seasons change is called a _____ .

5 A habitat that gets rain almost every day is a _____ .

6 Snow is on the ground for much of the year in the _____ .

Science Ideas

7 The Mojave Desert gets 5 inches of rain a year. Death Valley gets 2 inches of rain a year. How much more rain does the Mojave Desert get? Write a number sentence to solve.

8 Which of these animals does not live in a desert? Where does it live? How do you know?

rattlesnake

chipmunk

lizard

Inquiry Skill: Communicate

9 How does this animal's color help it stay safe? Write about it.

READ
A Science Project for George
by Jennifer Jacobson
Now You See It, Now You Don't
by Geof Smith

Did You Ever Wonder?

[INQUIRY SKILL] What kind of sounds do animals make? **Draw a conclusion** about why animals make them.

Did You Ever Wonder?

How do some ocean animals eat their food? A sea otter floats on its back. It uses a stone to open shellfish.

INQUIRY SKILL **Predict** how a fish gets what it needs in the ocean. Then read a book to find out.

Life in a Fresh Water Habitat

Get Ready

These ducks live in a pond. They spend much of their day in the water. How do you think ducks are able to stay dry?

Inquiry Skill

You **infer** when you use what you know to figure something out.

Explore Activity

How does a duck stay dry?

What you need

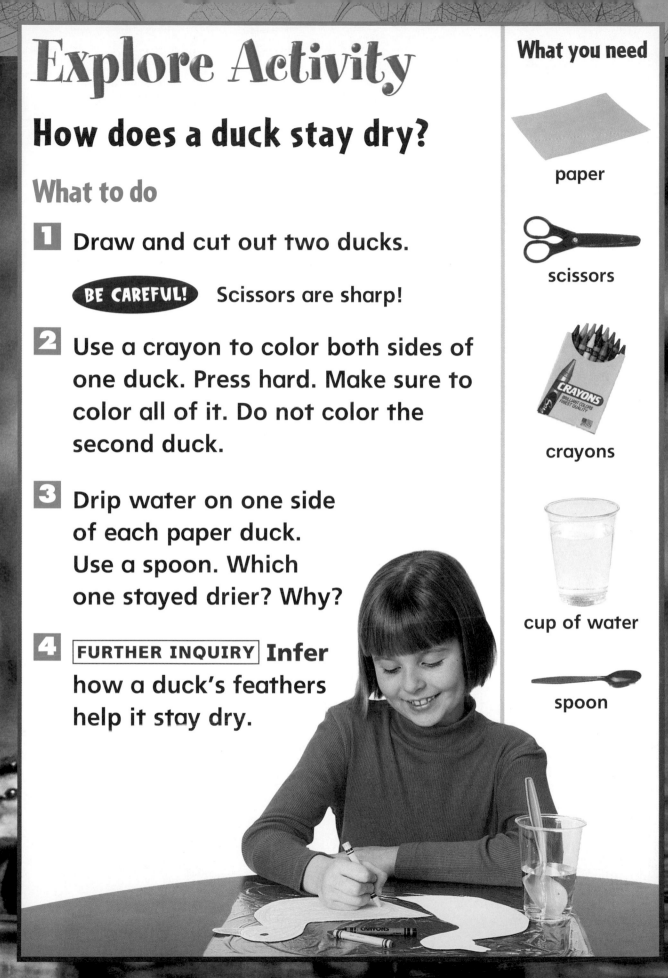

paper

scissors

crayons

cup of water

spoon

What to do

1 Draw and cut out two ducks.

BE CAREFUL! Scissors are sharp!

2 Use a crayon to color both sides of one duck. Press hard. Make sure to color all of it. Do not color the second duck.

3 Drip water on one side of each paper duck. Use a spoon. Which one stayed drier? Why?

4 **FURTHER INQUIRY** **Infer** how a duck's feathers help it stay dry.

cattails

What lives in a pond?

A **pond** is a fresh water habitat. Fresh water has little or no salt in it. Like water in a pool, pond water stays in one place. Plants grow in and around the pond. Some plants even float on the water.

bullfrog on water lily

Many pond fish eat water plants and insects. Birds make nests with pond grass. Beavers build homes with branches from nearby trees.

beaver

A pond can change through the year. Some ponds freeze in the winter. Fish swim below the ice. Turtles and frogs dig into the mud for warmth. Some insects sleep in the soil near the pond.

loon

mosquito

In summer a pond may dry up if there is not enough rain. Some pond animals leave and find new homes.

▷ **How do these animals get what they need in a pond habitat?**

perch swimming under ice

What lives in a stream?

A **stream** is a fresh water habitat with moving water. Salmon swim in streams. Sometimes they swim against the flow of the water to find a place to lay eggs.

salmon

otter

Otters find shelter on the sides of streams. Many insects and birds fly above the stream. They dive in the water to find food to eat. Some insects, like dragonflies, begin life in the water. Then they move to land.

gray wagtail

dragonfly

▷ How do these animals meet their needs?

Think and Write

1. How are ponds and streams alike? How are they different?

2. What do some pond animals do in the winter?

3. What are some ways animals find food in fresh water habitats?

 LOG ON Visit **www.science.mmhschool.com** to learn more about fresh water habitats.

Life in a Salt Water Habitat

Get Ready

Some animals live in a pond. Other animals live in the ocean. What kind of habitat do these two animals live in? How do you know?

Inquiry Skill

You **observe** when you use your senses to learn about the world around you.

Explore Activity

What lives in a salt water habitat?

What to do

1 Fill each container with two cups of water. Add two teaspoons of salt to one container. Mix it.

2 Add $\frac{1}{4}$ teaspoon of brine shrimp eggs to each container.

3 **Observe** what happens every day. Use a hand lens. Can brine shrimp grow in fresh water and salt water? Tell why or why not.

4 | FURTHER INQUIRY |
Observe how the brine shrimp change.

What you need

brine shrimp eggs

2 clear containers

spoon

salt

measuring spoon

measuring cup

hand lens

What lives in the ocean?

An **ocean** is a large, deep body of salt water. Oceans cover three-fourths of Earth. The salty water can be up to seven miles deep! It is deeper in some places than it is in others.

Most ocean animals and plants need salt water to live. They can not live in fresh water.

dolphin

eel

fish living in coral

Many fish search for sea plants or other fish to eat. Dolphins and whales also swim to find food. They are mammals, so they must come to the surface to breathe air.

starfish

Different plants and animals live in different parts of the ocean. Some animals live near the shore. Some live on the ocean floor.

▶ **How are all of these animals alike?**

lobster

octopus

What do ocean animals eat?

A **food web** is a group of several food chains that are connected. Here is one ocean food web.

Tiny plants and animals called plankton are food for many ocean animals. Plankton are a part of the ocean food web.

leopard seal

krill

emperor penguin

plankton

squid

Many fish and krill eat plankton. Larger fish, seals, and penguins eat these fish. Some whales then eat seals and penguins. The arrows in this picture show what is food for each animal.

▶ **What does the killer whale eat?**

killer whale

Think and Write

1. What is an ocean?

2. How deep can an ocean get in some places?

3. What is a food web?

MORE TO READ Read **The Magic School Bus on the Ocean Floor** by Joanna Cole.

Caring for Earth's Habitats

What if the ocean were covered with black slime? That is what happens when oil spills into the water. What do you think this oil spill will do to the bird and its habitat?

Inquiry Skill

You **predict** when you use what you know to tell what you think will happen.

Explore Activity

What can oil do to a bird's feathers?

What to do

1 Put the feather in the water. **Predict** what will happen if you pour oil into the water.

2 Pour oil into the water. Tell what happens to the feather.

3 Try to remove the oil. Use paper towels. Is it easy or difficult? Wash your hands.

4 FURTHER INQUIRY **Predict** how oil can make a bird sick. Then read a book to find out.

tray of water

feather

cup of oil

paper towels

How can we care for the water?

Pollution happens when harmful things are put in water, air, or land. It can hurt living things. We can not make new water, air, or land. That is why we must take care of them.

When there are too many harmful things in water, we can not use it. Animals can get sick. We can help keep water clean by picking up trash. We can tell others about the dangers of pollution. There are also laws against pollution.

▶ **How are these people caring for a water habitat?**

oil spill

Workers help clean up a bird after an oil spill.

How can we care for the air?

Some people burn leaves and trash to get rid of them. This causes air pollution. Cars and factories can cause air pollution, too. There are laws to help keep the air clean. We can help keep the air clean by riding bikes and walking.

 How are these people caring for air?

air pollution

How can we care for the land?

Every day trees are cut down to clear land for building. Many trees are also cut down for wood and paper. We can help care for the land by planting trees. Tree leaves give off oxygen for us to breathe. Tree roots keep soil from blowing or washing away. Planting trees also makes homes for animals.

planting trees

cleared land

We throw away tons of trash every year. Much of this trash goes to big pits in the ground called landfills. Landfills are getting too full to hold more trash.

landfill

We can cut down on waste. We can **recycle** paper, glass, cans, and plastic. Recycled waste can be made into new things and used again. People can make shoes, clothes, and toys from recycled plastic.

▷ **How are these people caring for the land?**

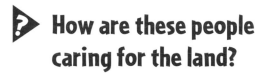

1. What is pollution?
2. How does recycling help the garbage problem?

recycling

HOME ACTIVITY What can you do to cut down on trash at home?

Go Fishing for Facts

Fish come in all shapes and sizes. They live all over the world. Learn about ocean fish. Read *Fishy Facts* by Anne Miranda.

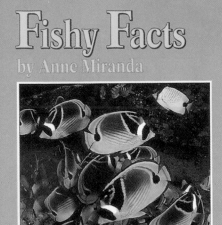

Fishy Facts
by Anne Miranda

Try This!

Use your library to find out more about fish. Pick one fish that you like. Draw it on one side of a piece of paper. Write your own fishy facts on the other side.

Science Newsroom CD-ROM Choose **Don't Be Dinner** to learn how animals hide.

Recycled Art

Do you think art can be made by only drawing or painting? Think again! Some artists use materials that would be trash.

Try This!

Gather things you no longer need. Think of a sculpture you want to make. Glue the pieces together to create your own recycled art!

Vocabulary

food web, B42

ocean, B40

pollution, B46

pond, B34

stream, B36

recycle, B49

Use each word once for items 1–6.

1 Many food chains together make up a ____ .

2 When harmful things are in water, air, or land, it is called ____ .

3 A fresh water habitat with moving water is called a ____ .

4 When you save cans so they can be made into new things, you ____ .

5 A fresh water habitat with water that stays in one place is called a ____ .

6 A large body of salt water is called an ____ .

Science Ideas

7 What do pond turtles do for warmth during winter?

8 What do beavers use to make their homes?

9 Do these plants and animals live in fresh water or salt water? List them in two groups.

crab

frog

lily pad

killer whale

READ
River Home by Susan Blackaby

Did You Ever Wonder? **INQUIRY SKILL** **Investigate** ways you can clean up the land, water, and air.

Melanie Stiassny
MARINE BIOLOGIST

Melanie Stiassny is a marine biologist. She studies oceans. Marine biologists have many questions about life in the oceans. More facts are known about the Moon than about our oceans!

Melanie travels to many places. Sometimes she discovers new kinds of fish, such as the Etia nguti (EE-tee-ah NEW-tee). The female fish keeps her young safe by holding them in her mouth.

Melanie knows that we must care for our oceans. She says we must not take too many fish out of the water. If we do, there may not be any left!

LOG ON Visit www.science.mmhschool.com to learn more about marine biologists and oceans.

This is the jaw of a tiger shark.

Think Big!

Why do you think we know more about the Moon than about our oceans?

Habitat Story

Choose a plant or animal that lives in a land habitat. Write a short story about your plant or animal. What does it need to live in its habitat? How does it get what it needs?

Water Animal Skit

Think of an animal that lives in a water habitat. Pretend you are that animal and act out a story.

UNIT C

Exploring Indiana

Exploring Indiana

Tornado Safety Tips

➤ **LOOK** for signs of danger.

➤ **LISTEN** to instructions from parents or teachers.

➤ **GO** to a safe place in your home or school.

How We Use Water

Water comes from a source. The source can be a lake, river, stream, or well. Some people even collect rain water. We use machines to move water to where it is needed.

Look at the pictures. To save plants or animals during a drought, or dry period, we can bring water through pipes or sprinklers.

ACTIVITY

■ Do you have a pet animal or grow plants in your classroom? Write down what you need to bring to plants and give to pets to keep them healthy.

■ Add drawings and make a guidebook for a friend on how to care for pets and plants.

Wind Moves Sand

Sand dunes are piles of windblown sand. Sand dunes are shaped by the wind. The dunes are formed by the direction and strength of the wind.

To protect dunes from wind, people build fences or plant bushes and grass. These act to slow down the wind. The roots of plants help hold the sand in place.

Fences placed along walkways keep people from walking on the dunes. They also trap windblown sand.

Indiana Test Prep

1 Which of the following is *not* a natural source of water for crops?

A rain

B streams

C rivers

D wind

2 What is a drought?

A a wet period

B a machine

C a dry period

D a sprinkler

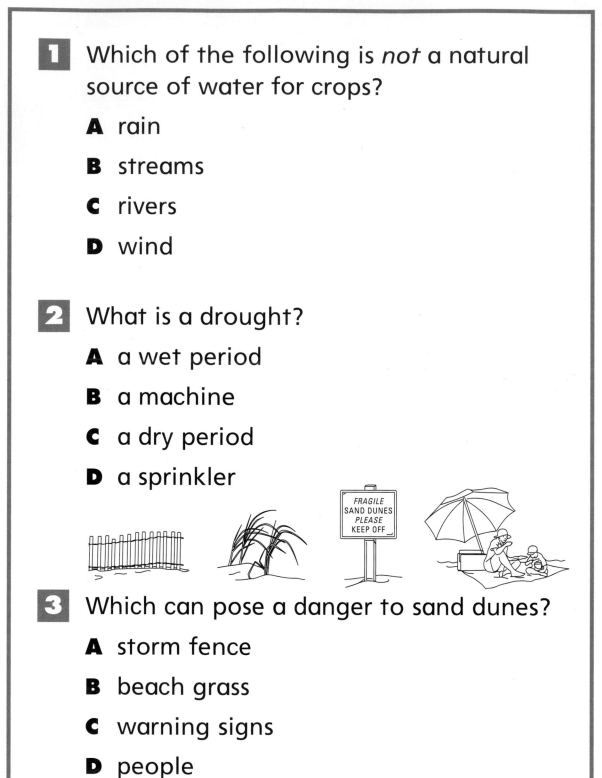

3 Which can pose a danger to sand dunes?

A storm fence

B beach grass

C warning signs

D people

UNIT C

Changes on Earth

LOOK!

What is happening in this picture? Where do you think the water is coming from? Take a good look.

Changes on Earth

Weather
and Other Earth Changes

Did You Ever Wonder?

How fast are tornado winds? Tornado wind speeds are often faster than 300 miles per hour!

INQUIRY SKILL **Predict** what might happen during a tornado.

C 3

1 Water and Our Weather

Get Ready

Have you ever been caught in the rain?
Did you know it was going to rain?
Could you tell by looking at the sky?

Inquiry Skill

You **draw a conclusion** when you use what you observe to explain what happens.

Explore Activity

Where does water for rain come from?

What to do

1 Put sand and some water in a cup.

BE CAREFUL! Wear goggles.

2 Put the cup into a plastic bag. Seal the bag. Put it in a sunny place.

3 Predict what will happen. After a few hours, observe the bag.

4 **FURTHER INQUIRY** Make another model. Put it in the dark. **Draw a conclusion** about what happened.

goggles

cup

sand

cup of water

plastic bag

How can water change?

Heat can change water. Heat causes water to **evaporate**, or change into gas. When water evaporates, it goes into the air. Water that goes into the air is called **water vapor**. You can not see water vapor.

Water vapor can be changed back into liquid. Cool air makes water vapor **condense**, or change into a liquid. On a cool morning, you may see tiny drops of water, called dew, on the grass. This is condensed water vapor.

Water condenses on a spider web.

 What happens to the water from the boy's sweatshirt?

What is the water cycle?

The water on Earth is always changing. It changes from ice to liquid to water vapor and back again. Water moves between the ground and the sky over and over. This movement of water is called the **water cycle**.

1 Heat from the Sun warms the land, air, and water. Then the water evaporates.

2 Water vapor rises. Then it cools and condenses into tiny drops of water.

3 The drops of water form clouds.

4 When the drops in the clouds get big enough, they fall to the ground as rain, snow, or hail. This is called **precipitation**.

5 Water returns to the lakes and oceans. The water cycle begins again.

? **What is the water that falls from clouds called?**

What are some special kinds of weather?

Weather always changes. Some weather can cause big changes on Earth. We can not be sure of what the weather will be like. But we can predict it.

If a lot of rain falls quickly, the ground can not soak up all the water. Too much water can make a river overflow. Heavy rain can cause floods.

A drought happens when a place does not get enough rain. The land dries up. Plants and animals can not get water.

flood

drought

hurricane

A hurricane is a very strong storm. It can cause floods and harm beaches.

A tornado is a storm with very fast winds that spin in circles. The winds can damage many things.

 How can weather change Earth?

Think and Write

1. What happens to water when it evaporates?

2. What is the water cycle?

3. What causes a flood?

LOG ON Visit www.science.mmhschool.com to learn more about weather.

tornado

Earth Can Change Slowly

Get Ready

Have you ever seen rocks like this? Rocks are very hard. Do you think you could change the shape of a rock? Tell how.

Inquiry Skill

You **communicate** when you share what you know.

Explore Activity

How can you change rocks?

What to do

1 Look at the rocks with a hand lens. Rub them on sandpaper. **Communicate** what happened.

2 Put the rocks inside the jar of water. Close the lid tightly. Shake the jar for a few minutes.

3 Look at the rocks. Communicate what happened.

4 **FURTHER INQUIRY**
How else could you change rocks? **Communicate** your ideas.

What you need

rocks

sandpaper

plastic jar of water

hand lens

How can rocks change?

Water and wind can wear down rocks. **Erosion** happens when worn down rocks are carried away. It may happen so slowly that you can not see it.

When water or ice rubs against rock, it wears away at the rock. Water can move small rocks. These rocks bump into each other and break off into smaller pieces.

Grand Canyon, Arizona

Wind can move sand. The sand rubs against rocks. The rubbing wears down the rocks bit by bit.

It has taken thousands of years for water and wind to wear down the rocks in these pictures.

Tell what happened to the rocks in these pictures.

Monument Valley, Utah

Bryce Canyon, Utah

How can soil and sand change?

Bits of rock that wear away from bigger rocks become soil and sand. Bits of dead plants and animals also become part of soil.

Water can erode soil and sand. Heavy rain can wash soil away. Ocean waves can carry away sand.

Waves carry away sand.

Wind blows soil away.

Wind can also erode soil and sand. Strong winds can blow soil and sand away. This may make a dust storm.

Plants help to keep soil and sand from eroding. Plant roots hold soil and sand in place. Then water and wind can not wash or blow soil and sand away easily.

▷ **How can plants help stop erosion?**

Plants keep soil and sand in place.

Think and Write

1. What is erosion?

2. Tell what soil is made of.

3. How can plants keep soil and sand from eroding?

HOME ACTIVITY Collect some rocks. Rub them together. Can any rocks be changed or scratched?

Earth Can Change Quickly

Get Ready

What happened to this road? What do you think might have caused this destruction?

Inquiry Skill

You **observe** when you use your senses to learn about something.

Explore Activity

How can Earth's surface change?

What to do

1 Put two halves of a pan together. Line them with foil. **BE CAREFUL!**

2 Make mud out of soil and water. Spread it in the pan.

3 Let the mud dry. Move the two sides of the pan quickly against each other.

4 **Observe** what happens. How did the surface change?

5 **FURTHER INQUIRY** Do the same activity with sand. **Observe** what happens.

What you need

foil

foil pan cut in half

bowl

water

soil

spoon

What is an earthquake?

An **earthquake** is a shaking of the ground. It is caused by a shift of Earth's surface, or crust. Earth's crust is made up of pieces called plates. These plates fit together like a puzzle. Sometimes the edges of two plates move or rub against each other. This can cause an earthquake.

▷ **How do earthquakes change Earth?**

An earthquake made this crack in the ground.

What is a landslide?

A **landslide** is a sudden movement of soil down a hill. Earthquakes sometimes cause landslides. Landslides may also happen when a lot of rainwater makes the soil heavy and slippery. The ground becomes weak and slides downhill.

▶ **How do landslides change Earth?**

What is a volcano?

A **volcano** is a mountain. It forms when hot, melted rock erupts through a hole in Earth's surface and builds up. The melted rock that flows out of the volcano is called lava. Lava becomes hard rock when it cools.

Volcanoes often form in places where Earth's plates rub against each other.

▷ **How can a volcano change Earth?**

The volcano erupts. Hot gases, lava, and ashes erupt from a hole in Earth's crust.

Hot rock builds up.

Mount St. Helens
April 1980

Mount St. Helens
May 18, 1980

After the volcano erupts, the lava cools into hard rock.

Mount St. Helens
June 1980

Years later, the volcano is no longer active. Plants begin to grow back and wildlife returns.

Mount St. Helens
1990

Think and Write

1. What happens to Earth's crust in an earthquake?

2. What is a volcano?

3. What happens when lava cools?

MORE TO READ

Read **Shake Rattle and Roll: The World's Most Amazing Earthquakes, Volcanoes, and Other Forces** by Spencer Christian.

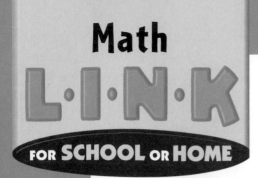

Make a Weather Chart

Look at the weather tools. How can you use them?

Try This!

Make a weather chart for the week. Use the tools to observe the weather in the morning and afternoon. How did the weather change each day? What weather patterns do you see?

Make Your Own Rocks

The southwestern United States is filled with beautiful rock formations. Read *Standing Up Country: A Land of Surprises* by Linnea Gentry to find out about some of them.

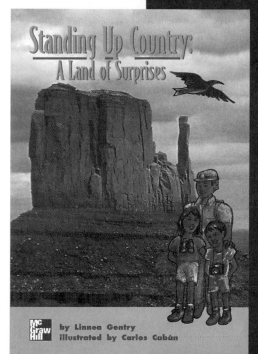

Standing Up Country:
A Land of Surprises

by Linnea Gentry
illustrated by Carlos Cabán

Try This!

Use clay to make rock shapes. They can look like the rocks in *Standing Up Country*. You can make shapes of your own, too.

Science Newsroom CD-ROM
Choose **The Water Cycle** to learn more about weather.

Chapter 5 Review

Vocabulary

condense, C7

earthquake, C20

erosion, C14

evaporate, C6

landslide, C21

precipitation, C9

volcano, C22

water cycle, C8

water vapor, C6

Use each word once for items 1–9.

1 Water that goes into the air is called ____ .

2 Heat causes liquid water to ____ , or change into gas.

3 Rain, snow, and hail are kinds of ____ .

4 Cool air makes water vapor ____ , or turn into liquid water.

5 Water moving between the ground, sky, and back again is called the ____ .

6 When worn down rocks are carried away by water, it is called ____ .

7 A shaking of the ground caused by the shifting of Earth's crust is an ____ .

8 A mountain made of cooled lava is a ____ .

9 A sudden movement of soil down a hill is a ____ .

Science Ideas

10 Which picture shows a drought?

A

B

Inquiry Skill: Draw a Conclusion

11 Draw a conclusion about how these rocks got their shapes.

READ
California Fire! by Sneed B. Collard III

Did You Ever Wonder?

INQUIRY SKILL **Predict** how people stay safe during a tornado. Then read a book to find out.

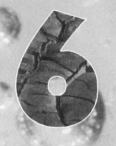

Earth
Yesterday and Today

Did You Ever Wonder?

How do we know what insects looked like in the time of dinosaurs? Whole insects have been found trapped in ancient tree sap.

INQUIRY SKILL **Compare** this insect to an insect that lives today.

C 29

Clues in Rocks

Get Ready

Do you like to find clues? Look at these animal tracks. What kind of animal do you think made them? How do you know?

Inquiry Skill

You **infer** when you use what you know to figure something out.

Explore Activity

clay

How can we get clues from prints?

What to do

1. Press a secret object into clay. Gently take the object away.

small objects

2. Make prints with two more objects.

3. Trade clay prints with a partner. **Infer** what objects made the shapes in your partner's clay. What clues did you use to figure them out?

4. **FURTHER INQUIRY** **Infer** how scientists use prints to learn about animals.

C 3

What are fossils?

Fossils are what is left of living things from the past. Some fossils are prints of plants or animals. Other fossils are parts of things that were once living. These parts can be bones or teeth. Fossils can also be footprints, tracks, or nests that animals left behind.

dinosaur footprint in rock

plant fossil in rock

dinosaur tooth fossil

dinosaur fossil in rock

Scientists find fossils in many places. Many fossils are found in rock. A fossil may even be a whole animal or plant trapped and saved in ice, tar, or amber. Amber is hardened tree sap.

 What are some different kinds of fossils?

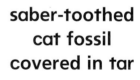

insect fossil in amber

saber-toothed cat fossil covered in tar

How are fossils formed?

Many fossils form when living things are buried. Most fossils are found in rocks that form very slowly in layers. Scientists can tell how old a fossil is when they know the age of the rock layer it is in.

 Where are most fossils found?

How a Fossil Forms

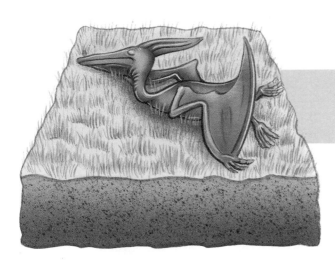

1. An animal dies. Layers of mud, soil, or clay bury the remains of the animal.

2. More mud layers build up. The soft parts of the animal rot away. The hard bones and teeth are left.

Think and Write

1. What are fossils?

2. Tell how some fossils form.

3. Do you think fossils are still being formed today? Tell why or why not.

HOME ACTIVITY Press your hand into clay. Let the clay dry. What does the handprint tell about you?

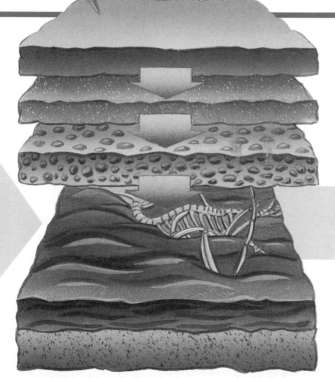

3 The mud, bones, and teeth slowly change to rock. The hard parts of the animal are saved.

4 Millions of years later, the fossil is found.

Putting the Clues Together

Get Ready

Have you ever worked on a puzzle? Scientists work on puzzles, too. They put together fossil bones to show what an animal looked like.

Inquiry Skill

You **make a model** when you build something that shows what the real thing is like.

Explore Activity

Which bones fit together?

What to do

1 Look at the dinosaur bones. What do you think the dinosaur will look like? Draw a picture.

2 Cut out the bones.

> **BE CAREFUL!** Scissors are sharp.

3 Make a **model** of the dinosaur. Tape the bones together. Compare your picture and the model.

4 FURTHER INQUIRY Make a model of what the dinosaur looked like when it was alive.

What you need

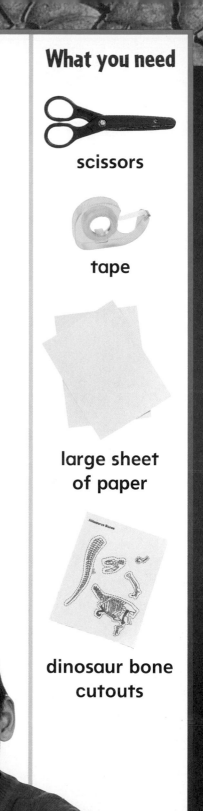

scissors

tape

large sheet of paper

dinosaur bone cutouts

How do scientists work with fossils?

Paleontologists are scientists who study things that lived long ago. They find and study fossils.

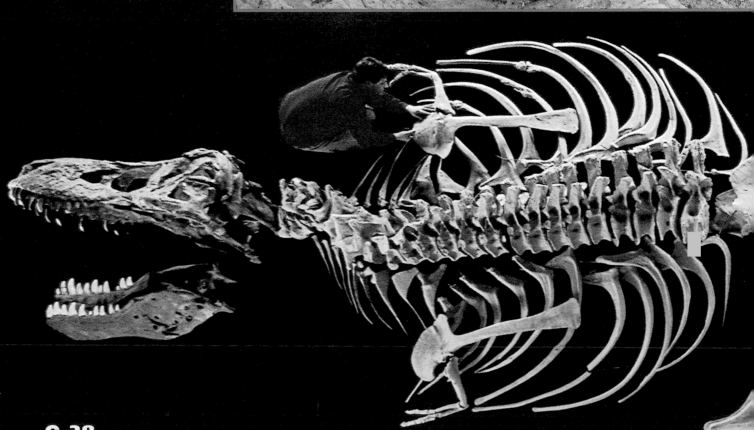

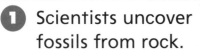
1 Scientists uncover fossils from rock.

Scientists put together a dinosaur **skeleton**, or a full set of bones. Skeletons help scientists learn about animals. They can tell how big the animal was and how the animal may have moved.

▶ **What can this fossil skeleton tell us about the dinosaur?**

2 They clean the fossil pieces. They rebuild some fossil bones from broken pieces.

3 Scientists put the fossil skeleton together.

Skeleton of Tyrannosaurus Rex

What clues do scientists get from animals today?

No one knows for sure what dinosaurs were like. Scientists use what they know about animals today to learn about dinosaurs. They compare fossil bones to the bones of living animals. This helps them put fossil bones together. It also helps them figure out how dinosaurs may have lived.

The stegosaurus had flat plates on its back and a spiked tail. Scientists think these things helped it stay safe.

stegosaurus

lizard

pterodactyl

heron

The pterodactyl had large wings and a long beak. It may be a relative of today's birds.

Scientists compare fossil teeth to the teeth of animals today. They know that today's meat eaters have sharp teeth. They also know that today's plant eaters have flat teeth. This helps scientists figure out what dinosaurs ate.

allosaurus

The allosaurus had sharp claws, a large jaw, and sharp teeth. Scientists think it was a meat eater.

▶ Tell how these dinosaurs are like some animals of today.

alligator

How did dinosaurs live?

Dinosaurs lived on Earth millions of years ago. They lived on land.

Earth was very different then. The air and oceans were warm. The land had many swamps and giant forests.

pterodactyl

apatosaurus

allosaurus

Fossil footprints show that some dinosaurs lived in groups. This helped them to stay safe or hunt other animals. Tracks can show the kinds of prey meat-eating dinosaurs chased.

Some dinosaurs laid eggs. Scientists have found fossil nests. The nests had fossil eggs and young dinosaurs in them.

? How do we know that dinosaurs laid eggs?

stegosaurus

Think and Write

1. Why are dinosaur bones like pieces of a puzzle?

2. What can fossil teeth tell us about an animal?

3. Why did some dinosaurs travel in groups?

MORE TO READ

Read **A Dinosaur Named Sue: The Find of a Century** by Fay Robinson.

Life on Earth Changes

Get Ready

A giant panda needs to eat up to 20 pounds of bamboo a day. That's as much as 60 heads of lettuce! What do you think would happen if a panda could not find any bamboo?

Inquiry Skill

You **infer** when you use what you know to figure something out.

Explore Activity

What happens when animals can not meet their needs?

index cards labeled Food, Water, or Shelter

What to do

1 Line up. Take three cards.

2 If the cards say Food, Water, and Shelter, go to the back of the line. If you are missing one, sit down.

3 Play for four more rounds. What happens to the number of players each round?

4 FURTHER INQUIRY Infer what happens to animals when they can not meet their needs.

Why do living things become extinct?

When something is **extinct**, it has died out. That means none of its kind is living anywhere on Earth. Animals become extinct if they can not get the food, water, or shelter they need.

Long ago, many living things died out. They may have become extinct because of disease or big changes on Earth.

This is a drawing of a saber-toothed cat. It became extinct eleven thousand years ago.

This is a model of a triceratops. This dinosaur lived on Earth millions of years ago.

Today living things still become extinct. Many times people are the cause. People destroy habitats by cutting down forests and building on land where animals make their homes. People also hunt animals.

The dodo, shown in this drawing, became extinct in 1681.

 Why are these animals extinct?

This is a model of a woolly mammoth. The mammoth lived 20 thousand years ago.

The golden toad, last seen in 1989, is thought to be extinct.

pitcher plant

white
rhinoceros

aye aye

What living things are endangered?

When living things are **endangered**, they are in danger of becoming extinct. They need to be kept safe in order to live. Today it is against the law to harm an endangered animal or plant.

We can help these animals and plants. We can keep the places where they live safe and clean.

manatee

▶ **Why are these living things endangered?**

lowland gorilla

Why is there hope for endangered life?

Some plants and animals have come back from near extinction. Some animals, such as the American bison, the bald eagle, and the humpback whale, are growing in numbers. This is because people have tried to keep the habitats of these animals safe. People have also stopped hunting them.

American bison

bald eagle

 Why is it important to protect all habitats?

Think and Write

1. What may have caused dinosaurs to become extinct?

2. What can we do today to save endangered animals?

 LOG ON Visit www.science.mmhschool.com to find out more about extinct and endangered animals.

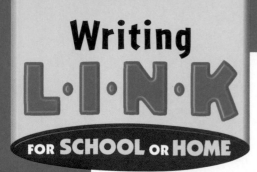

Make a Dinosaur Big Book

Do you have a favorite dinosaur? Find a book about dinosaurs. Pick one you would like to learn about.

The Big Book of Dinosaurs

Try This!

Writing That Gives Information
Draw a picture of a dinosaur on a big piece of paper. Write facts about it. Then join with others to make a big book.

Triceratops had 3 horns. It ate plants.

Collect and Sort Rocks

Rocks come in all shapes and sizes. Collect rocks and find out how many ways you can sort them.

small

medium

large

Try This!

Look at the rocks. Find three ways to describe your rocks. Then sort them. Estimate how many rocks are in each group. Then count the rocks and write how many are in each group.

Science Newsroom CD-ROM
Choose **Dino Match** to learn more about dinosaurs.

Vocabulary

endangered, C48

extinct, C46

fossils, C32

paleontologist, C38

skeleton, C39

Use each word once for items 1–5.

1 A scientist who studies living things from the past is a ____ .

2 Living things that have died out and no longer live on Earth are ____ .

3 Living things that are close to becoming extinct are ____ .

4 Remains of living things from the past are ____ .

5 A full set of bones is a ____ .

Science Ideas

6 How are the animals in these pictures alike and different?

7 What can you infer from the shapes of this dinosaur's teeth?

READ
Saving Our Animals
by Billy Goodman

Did You Ever Wonder? INQUIRY SKILL **Investigate** where one dinosaur lived. How did it meet its needs?

Ji Qiang

GEOLOGIST

Ji Qiang (ZHEE CHAHNG) is a geologist. He studies rocks to learn about Earth's past. Qiang studied the fossil of a dinosaur that had feathers.

To dig up fossils, Qiang uses a kind of hammer. It is sharp on one end. It is flat on the other. Qiang also uses a soft brush to remove dust. This does not hurt the fossil.

LOG ON Visit www.science.mmhschool.com to learn more about geologists.

Animals that change over time may survive changes on Earth. Fossils tell Qiang about these changes. Qiang compares dinosaurs to living animals. He looks for clues that can teach us how animals lived long ago.

This is a model of a Sinosauropteryx.

Think Big!

How is a fossil like a piece of a puzzle?

C 55

Earth Changes

Write a story about a change on Earth you read about. Be sure to answer these questions:

- Is it a fast change or a slow change?
- How does the change happen?

Make a cover for your story. Give your story a title.

Dinosaur Home

Make a model of a dinosaur and its habitat. Choose any dinosaur you want. Use a shoe box to make your model. Show what kind of teeth your animal has. What kind of food does it eat? Show the animals or plants that it eats.

UNIT D

Exploring Indiana

Exploring Indiana

LOOK!

This cardinal looks for food in the winter. How does the cardinal stay warm?

Animals in Winter

Birds, deer, and chipmunks can survive cold temperatures by staying warm and finding food. How do these animals stay warm? What do they eat?

Sleeping bats

Chipmunks and bats sleep through a cold winter. Before winter comes, they eat more and store energy as body fat.

During winter, they keep still in a safe place. They use their stored fat to keep warm. They become active again when the weather warms up.

Chipmunk

ACTIVITY

Look at these sentence starters. Finish each one.

■ Chipmunks get ready for winter by…

■ When winter comes chipmunks…

The Moon

On clear nights, you can see the Moon in the sky. The Moon is smaller than Earth. The Moon glows as it reflects light from the Sun. There is no air or water on the Moon.

The Moon is the brightest object in the sky, except for the Sun. The next time you are outside, day or night, look for the Moon. What makes it possible for us to see the Moon?

ACTIVITY

The shape of the Moon seems to change over 28 days. Describe the Moon as it changes shape.

Indiana Test Prep

1 Which animal mostly stays still during winter?

    A Eagle

    B Deer

    C Blue Bird

    D Chipmunk

2 The brightest object in the night sky is

    A the Moon.

    B the Sun.

    C Earth.

    D Mars.

3 Why does the Moon glow?

UNIT D
The Sun and Its Family

LOOK!

The Sun gives light
to all of the planets.
Where is the Sun
in this picture?
Take a good look.

The Sun and Its Family

Vocabulary

rotate, D6

axis, D6

Sun, D7

orbit, DI2

equator, DI6

Did You Ever Wonder?

What would Earth be like without the Sun? It would be so dark and so cold that nothing would be able to live.

INQUIRY SKILL **Communicate** how the Sun is a part of your life.

1 Day and Night

Atlanta at night

Get Ready

How are these two pictures different? How does day change to night? What kind of model could you make to show how this happens on Earth?

Atlanta during the day

Inquiry Skill

You make a model when you show how something happens.

Explore Activity

How does day change to night?

What to do

1 Use the ball to **make a model** of Earth. Push the pencil through the ball. Press the paper clip into the side. **BE CAREFUL!**

2 Use the flashlight to act like the Sun. Have a partner shine it at the paper clip. Where is it day on your model?

3 Slowly spin the ball with the pencil. How does day change to night?

4 **FURTHER INQUIRY** **Make a model** without the flashlight. What would Earth be like with no Sun?

How does Earth rotate?

Earth **rotates**, or spins, like a top. You can't feel it, but it is happening right now. Earth always spins in the same direction.

Earth rotates on a line through its center called an **axis**. Earth's axis is an imaginary line that goes from the North Pole to the South Pole.

axis

model of Earth

▷ **What does Earth do when it rotates?**

What is the Sun like?

As Earth rotates, the **Sun** shines on it. The Sun is a star. It is the closest star to Earth. The Sun gives Earth light and heat.

The Sun is huge. More than a million Earths could fit inside of it. The Sun looks small because it is 93 million miles away.

▷ **What does Earth get from the Sun?**

Sun

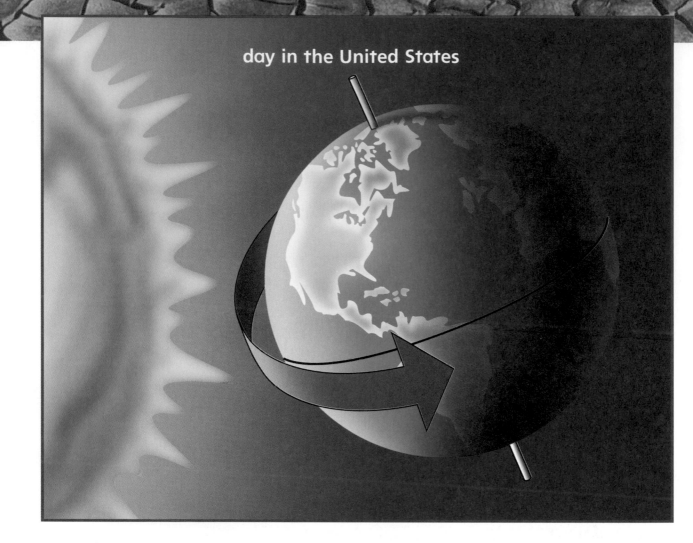

day in the United States

What causes day and night?

It seems as if the Sun is always moving across the sky. It looks as if the Sun rises in the east and sets in the west. But the Sun does not move. Earth's rotation causes day and night.

As Earth rotates, our part of Earth gets light, then dark. The Sun always shines, but it only lights half of Earth at a time. The half facing the Sun has light. The other half is dark. It takes 24 hours for Earth to rotate all the way around.

night in the United States

▶ **When it is daytime in the United States, what time of day is it on the other side of Earth?**

Think and Write

1. Why does the Sun look small?

2. What happens when Earth rotates?

3. How long does it take Earth to rotate one full time?

LOG ON Visit **www.science.mmhschool.com** to learn more about day and night.

Seasons

Get Ready

The same place can have different weather at different times of the year. Which picture shows Earth getting more light and heat from the Sun?

Inquiry Skill

You **compare** when you observe how things are alike and different.

Explore Activity

How do the seasons change through the year?

What to do

1 Divide a plate into four equal parts. Label them winter, spring, summer, and fall. Write them in order.

2 What do you like to do each season? Draw a picture in each part.

3 Cut one quarter out of your second plate. Place it on top of the first plate. Connect them with a fastener.

BE CAREFUL! Scissors are sharp.

4 Turn the top plate clockwise.

5 **FURTHER INQUIRY**

Compare the weather in winter and spring.

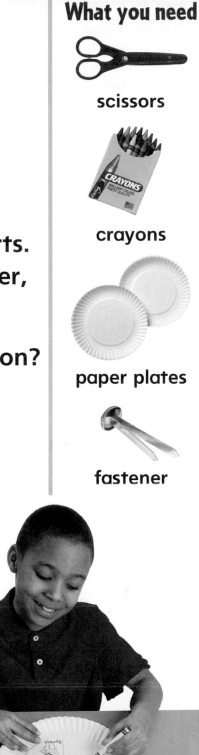

How does Earth move around the Sun?

As Earth rotates, it also travels around the Sun. The path Earth takes around the Sun is called its **orbit**. Earth always travels around the Sun in the same orbit. It takes Earth 365 days to travel once around the Sun.

Earth leans a little to one side. Because of this, half of Earth is always tilted toward the Sun. The other half is tilted away from the Sun. As Earth travels in its orbit, the side that tilts toward the Sun changes.

▷ **What is an orbit?**

fall

winter

Why do seasons change?

We have winter when our part of Earth is tilted away from the Sun. In winter less sunlight hits our part. So we get less light and heat.

summer

When we have summer, our part of Earth is tilted toward the Sun. More sunlight hits our part. So our part of Earth gets more light and heat.

▶ **Why does our part of Earth get less light and heat in winter?**

spring

What are seasons like in other places?

The **equator** is an imaginary line across the middle of Earth. It separates the northern part of Earth from the southern part. When it is summer in the northern part of Earth, it is winter in the southern part.

June 21st

United States, North America

June 21st

Argentina, South America

equator

Places near the equator do not have very different seasons. They have the same weather most of the year. This is because the amount of sunlight that hits the equator stays about the same all year.

June 21st

Venezuelan rain forest near the equator

▶ **What will the seasons be like in each place in December?**

Think and Write

1. What is an orbit?

2. Why does one part of Earth get more light and heat in the summer?

3. When it is winter above the equator, what season is it below the equator?

MORE TO READ

Read **Learn About the Changing Seasons** by Dr. Heidi Gold-Dworkin.

Go on a Sunset Walk

You know that the Sun always rises and sets. Sunsets can be beautiful! Read *Sunset Surprise* by Gail Tuchman.

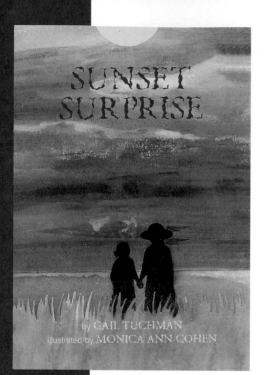

Try This!

With an adult, find a place where you can watch the sunset. Bring a watch with you. How long is it from the time the Sun begins to set until it is dark? Draw a picture of what you see.

Measuring Shadows

Did you know that shadows can tell you about the time of day? Shadows have different lengths depending on where the Sun is in the sky.

Try This!

Stand in exactly the same place at different times during the day. Have a person mark the top of your shadow with chalk. Estimate how long the shadow is each time. Then measure it. Record the numbers on a graph. What pattern do you see?

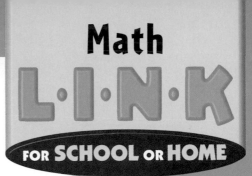

Chapter 7 Review

Vocabulary

axis, D6

equator, D16

orbit, D12

rotates, D6

Sun, D7

Use each word once for items 1–5.

1 The closest star to Earth is the ____ .

2 Once every 24 hours, Earth spins around, or ____ .

3 Earth spins on a line through its center that is called an ____ .

4 The path an object takes as it moves around another object is an ____ .

5 The imaginary line that separates the northern part of Earth from the southern part is the ____ .

Science Ideas

6 What makes the Sun look as if it moves across the sky?

7 This place has the same weather most of the year. What is it near?

Inquiry Skill: Make a Model

8 This ball is a model of Earth. The paper clip shows where you live. What is the flashlight a model of?

Did You Ever Wonder? INQUIRY SKILL **Investigate** what would happen to plants if there were no Sun.

Moon, Stars, and Planets

Did You Ever Wonder?

What does the surface of the Moon look like? It has big holes called craters.

INQUIRY SKILL How could you **make** a **model** of the moon? How could you make craters in your model?

The Moon

Get Ready

This picture was taken from space. It shows part of Earth and its nearest neighbor. What do you think that neighbor is? Why does it shine in space?

Inquiry Skill

You **infer** when you use what you know to figure something out.

Explore Activity

What makes the Moon shine?

What to do

large foam ball

small foam ball

foil

flashlight

1 Use the flashlight to act like the Sun. Use the large ball to act like Earth. Wrap the small ball in foil. Use this ball to act like the Moon.

2 Make the classroom dark.

3 Move the Moon in a circle around Earth. Observe what happens.

4 FURTHER INQUIRY
Infer what makes the Moon shine.

What is the Moon like?

The **Moon** is Earth's nearest neighbor. It is a ball of rock that orbits Earth. The Moon takes about 27 days to make one full orbit.

The Moon is the brightest object in the night sky. But the Moon can not make its own light or heat. It looks like it shines because the Sun's light bounces off of it.

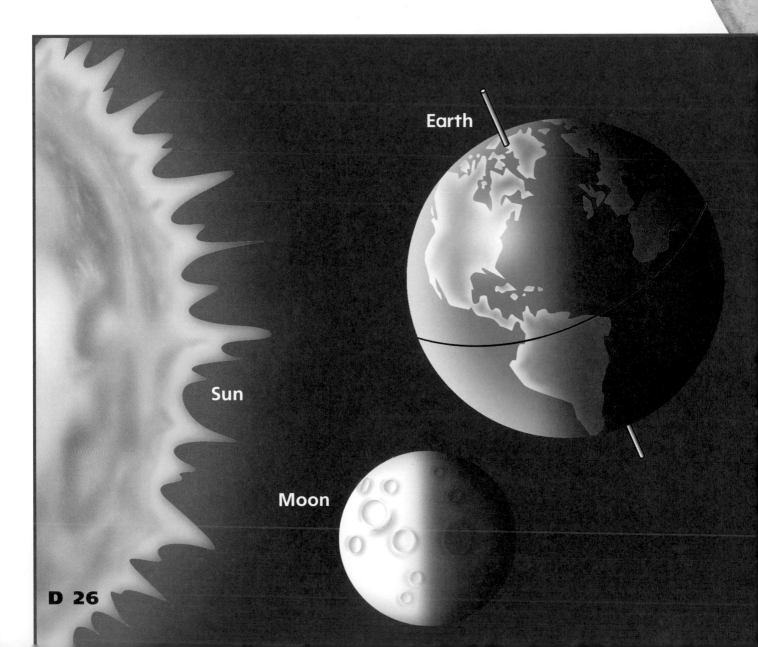

Earth

Sun

Moon

The Moon's surface is dry. It is covered with rocks and dust. The Moon has mountains and flat areas. It also has many **craters**, or large holes. Most craters were made by rocks from space that crashed into the Moon.

▶ **Why does the moon shine?**

What does the Moon look like during one night?

The Moon seems to move across the sky during the night. It rises in the east and sets in the west. Like the Sun, the Moon seems to move because Earth rotates. The Moon rises and sets as Earth turns.

7:30 P.M.

In early evening, the Moon is not very bright in the sky. Then the sky gets darker. The Moon seems to become brighter. The Moon looks brightest when the night sky is darkest.

 What makes the Moon look as if it is moving across the sky?

11:00 P.M.

Think and Write

1. What is the Moon?

2. How does the Moon shine?

3. Why does the Moon seem to rise and set?

HOME ACTIVITY Make Moon craters. Put flour on the bottom of a deep pan. Drop a few small rocks onto the pan.

The Moon Changes

Get Ready

Have you ever taken a good look at the night sky? Sometimes the Moon looks like a small sliver in the sky. Then, after a few days, it seems to look bigger. What do you think happens after that?

Inquiry Skill

You put things **in order** when you tell what comes first, next, and last.

Explore Activity

How does the Moon seem to change over time?

What you need

calendar

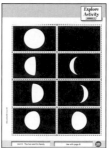
Moon worksheet

scissors

glue stick

What to do

1. Observe the Moon for a month.

2. Each night, draw in the calendar how the Moon looks.

3. **FURTHER INQUIRY** Cut out the Moon shapes from the worksheet. Glue them **in order**. Start with the full Moon.

Why does the Moon seem to change shape?

The Moon does not really get bigger and change shape. The lit part of the Moon that we can see changes. The different shapes of the Moon that we can see as it travels around Earth are called **phases**.

The first phase is the new Moon. We can not see the new Moon because its lit side is facing away from Earth.

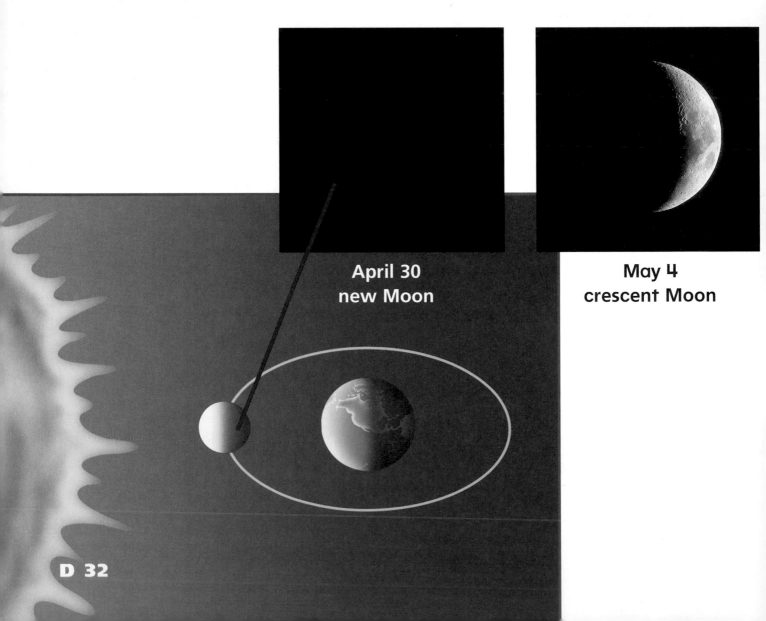

April 30
new Moon

May 4
crescent Moon

Each night after the new Moon, we can see more of the Moon. After about 7 nights, the Moon is about one-fourth of the way through its orbit. We can see half of the Moon's lit side.

After about 14 nights, we can see a full Moon. When the Moon is full, Earth is between the Sun and the Moon. We can see all of the Moon's lit side.

▶ **Why can't we see the new Moon?**

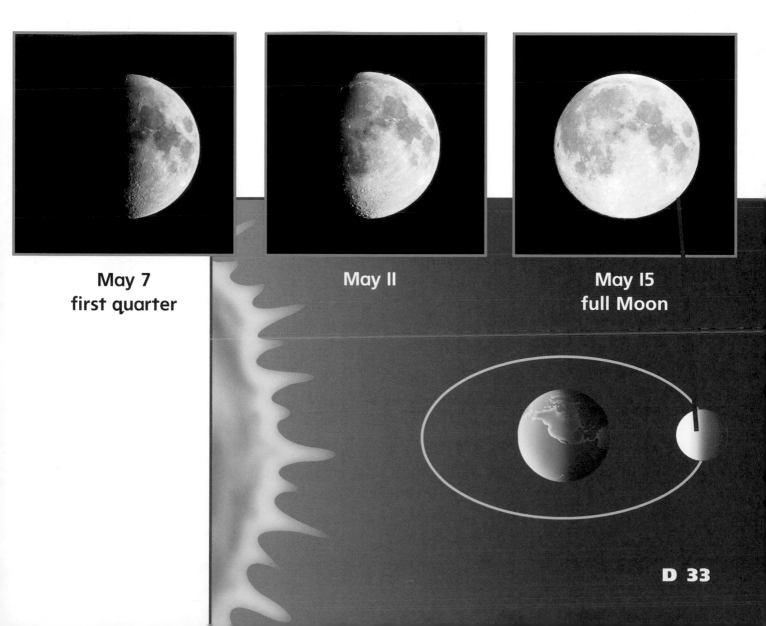

May 7
first quarter

May 11

May 15
full Moon

What happens as the Moon seems to get smaller?

Each night after the full Moon, we see less of the Moon. After about 21 nights, the Moon is three-fourths through its orbit. We can see the other half of the Moon's lit side.

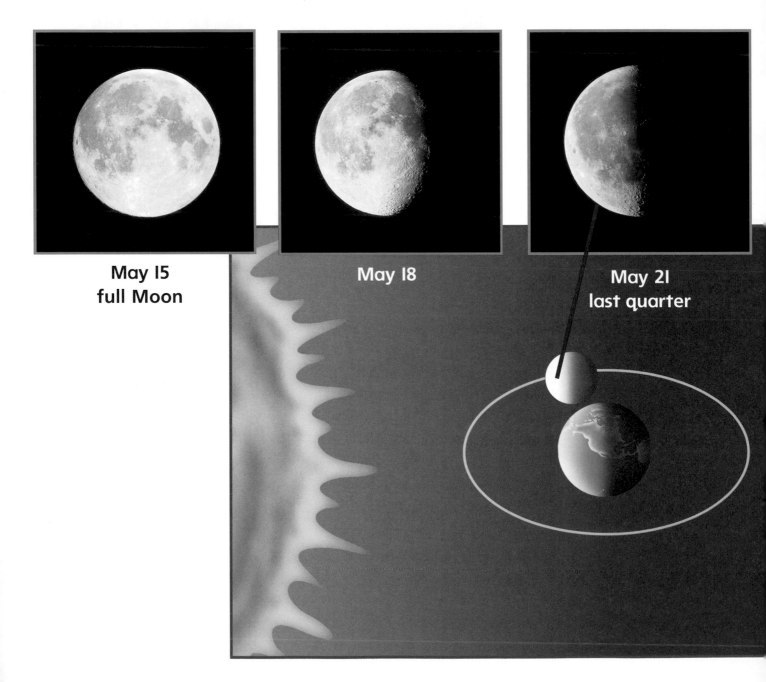

May 15
full Moon

May 18

May 21
last quarter

After about a month, the Moon seems to disappear again. It is the new Moon phase. It takes about a month for the Moon to change from a new Moon to a full Moon and back again.

▶ **What happens after we see the next new Moon?**

May 25

**May 28
new Moon**

Think and Write

1. Why do we see different shapes of the Moon?

2. What seems to happen to the Moon's shape right after the new Moon?

3. In which phase is the Moon closest to the Sun?

LOG ON Visit **www.science.mmhschool.com** to learn more about the Moon.

LESSON 5 Stars

Get Ready

The night sky is filled with stars. Look at the stars in this picture. Are some stars brighter than others? Are some stars bigger than others?

Inquiry Skill

You **observe** when you use your senses to learn about something.

Explore Activity

What does the night sky look like?

What to do

1 Wrap a box in black paper. Poke holes on one side to show part of the night sky.

> **BE CAREFUL!** Scissors are sharp.

2 Cut a hole in one end. Turn off the lights. Shine a flashlight into the box.

3 Observe your box and talk about what you see with others.

4 FURTHER INQUIRY Observe the night sky for a week. What do you see each night?

D 37

What you need

cereal box

black paper

tape

flashlight

scissors

What are stars?

A **star** is a hot ball of gases. Stars make their own light and heat. They look tiny because they are so far away. The biggest stars are much bigger than our closest star, the Sun. Stars are always in the sky.

Stars seem to move from east to west as Earth rotates. There are too many stars to count! Scientists look at them through tools called telescopes.

telescope

Stars may have different sizes and brightness. They may look bright because they are bigger or hotter than other stars near them. Stars also look bright when they are closer to Earth.

Stars have different colors. The hottest stars are blue. The coolest stars are red.

 How many stars are there in the sky?

blue star

red star

What are constellations?

Long ago people saw that groups of stars seemed to form pictures. A **constellation** is a star pattern that makes a picture. People gave some constellations names. Constellations are named after animals, objects, and people from old stories.

Scorpius looks like a scorpion to some people.

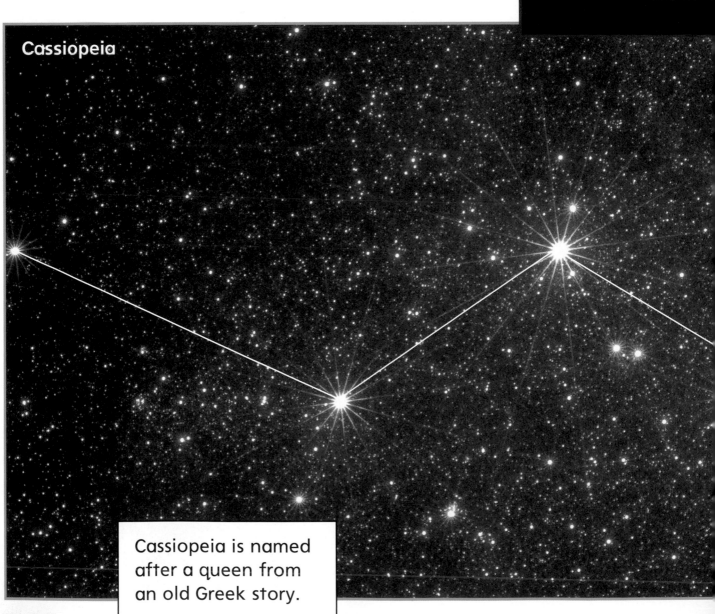

Cassiopeia

Cassiopeia is named after a queen from an old Greek story.

Scorpius

Little Dipper

Big Dipper

The Big Dipper and Little Dipper got their names because they are shaped like tools that hold water.

❓ How did constellations get their names?

Think and Write

1. Why do some stars look brighter than others?

2. What can you use to see objects in the night sky more clearly?

3. What is a constellation?

 **MORE TO READ**

Read **The Night Sky (One Small Square)** by Donald M. Silver.

LESSON 6 Planets

Get Ready

This is Jupiter. It takes about 12 Earth years for this planet to orbit the Sun! How could you show how planets move in space?

Inquiry Skill

You **make a model** when you make something to show a place or thing.

Explore Activity

How are orbits alike and different?

chair

masking tape

What to do

1 Put a chair, labeled Sun, in the center of the room.

2 Tape a line from the chair to a wall. Number the tape I to 9. Have each person line up on a number.

3 **Make a model** of an orbit. Each person walks in a circle around the chair. Take the same-size steps. Count your steps together. Compare the orbits.

4 **FURTHER INQUIRY** Now use clay to **make a model**. Show how planets orbit the Sun.

What is the solar system?

The **solar system** includes the Sun, nine **planets**, and their moons. A planet is a huge object that travels around the Sun. It does not make its own light or heat. Each planet has its own orbit, or path, around the Sun.

Venus

Sun

Mercury

Earth

Mars

Saturn

Some planets are close to the Sun. Others are far away. The planets closer to the Sun have shorter orbits. The planets farther from the Sun have longer orbits. It takes them more time to travel around the Sun.

▶ **Which planet has the shortest orbit?**

Jupiter

Neptune

Uranus

Pluto

What are the planets like?

You may not see the planets, but they are always in the sky. Scientists have put the planets into two groups. The first four planets are closest to the Sun. These are called the inner planets. They are all solid balls of rock.

Mercury
Mercury is the closest planet to the Sun. It is rocky and has many craters like our Moon.

Venus
Venus is covered with thick yellow clouds. These clouds trap the Sun's heat. This makes Venus the hottest planet.

Earth
Earth is the planet on which we live. It has water and air. Earth is the only place we know where there is life. It has one moon.

Mars
Mars has a red, rocky surface. It has two moons. Space missions have traveled to Mars to look for signs of life.

Jupiter
Jupiter is the largest planet. It has clouds and rings of dust. Jupiter has 28 moons that we know of.

The outer planets are farthest from the Sun. Scientists think that some outer planets do not have solid surfaces.

▷ **How are the inner planets alike?**

Saturn
Saturn is nearly as big as Jupiter. It has large rings made of ice. It may have over 20 moons.

Uranus
Uranus is a blue-green color. It is very cold. Uranus has thin rings made of ice and dust. It has 20 moons and may have more.

Neptune
Neptune is the blue planet. It has thin rings. Neptune has at least eight moons.

Pluto
Pluto is the smallest planet. It is the coldest. It has the longest orbit. Pluto is made of rock and ice. It has one moon.

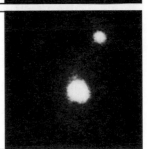

How do we learn about the planets?

In 1957, *Sputnik*, the first spacecraft, was launched. Since then, thousands of spacecraft have traveled into space. Twelve people have also walked on the Moon. People who explore space are called astronauts.

Spacecraft called space probes teach us about the planets. They carry tools that help us explore space.

 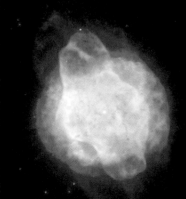

These are pictures taken by the Hubble Space Telescope.

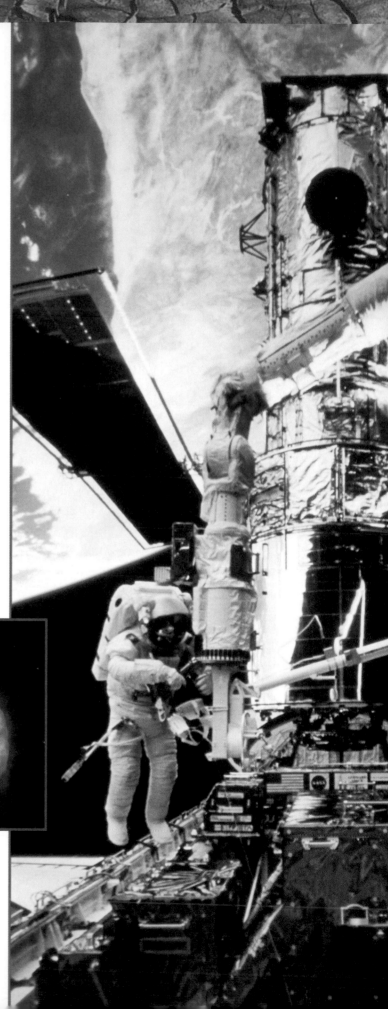

In 1997, the space probe *Mars Pathfinder* landed on Mars. It took pictures and collected rocks.

The *Galileo* was a space probe that helped us learn about Venus and Jupiter.

 **What is a space probe?**

This astronaut is fixing the Hubble Space Telescope. It takes pictures of objects that are very far away.

Think and Write

1. How many planets are in our solar system?

2. Which planet has the shortest orbit? the longest orbit?

3. What are some ways we learn about space?

 **MORE TO READ**

Read **Children of the Sun** by Arthur John L'Hommedieu.

Draw the Night Sky

Look at the night sky on a clear night. Do you see any constellations? Can you tell what phase the Moon is in?

Try This!

Draw what you see in the night sky. Use black paper and white chalk or crayons. You can draw pictures at different times of the month. Compare what you see.

Star Stories

There are many stories about how people long ago thought the night sky came to be. Some stories tell why the Moon changes shape. Others tell why some stars shine brighter than others.

Why the North Star is so Bright

Try This!

Writing a Story Tell why the stars and planets are in the sky. Write a story about the night sky. Then draw pictures for your story.

 Science Newsroom CD-ROM Choose **Constellations** to learn more about the night sky.

Chapter 8 Review

Vocabulary

constellation, D40

craters, D27

Moon, D26

phases, D32

planet, D44

solar system, D44

star, D38

Use each word once for items 1–7.

1 A large ball of rock that orbits Earth is the ____ .

2 Large holes in the Moon are ____ .

3 The different shapes of the Moon that we can see are called ____ .

4 A hot ball of gases is a ____ .

5 A group of stars that makes a picture is a ____ .

6 A huge object that travels around the Sun is a ____ .

7 The Sun, nine planets, and their moons make up the ____ .

Science Ideas

8 Tell how we learn about the night sky.

9 As planets get farther from the Sun, what happens to their orbits?

Inquiry Skill: Predict

10 Look at the pictures from left to right. Predict what will come next. Draw a picture.

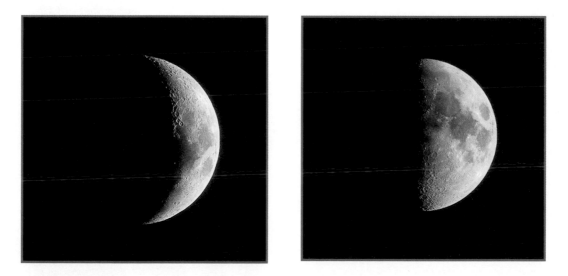

Did You Ever Wonder? ⎡INQUIRY SKILL⎤ People have walked on the Moon. **Communicate** what they brought with them and why.

Space Life

Astronauts can not feel gravity in space. That is why they float. What is life in space like for astronauts?

Astronauts work hard. They fix telescopes and satellites in space. They investigate planets and stars.

It is hard to eat in space. Astronauts eat sticky foods so crumbs do not float around. The crumbs can get into their eyes.

How do astronauts have fun? They watch movies and read. They use machines that help them run and ride a bike.

Sleeping can be hard in space. Some astronauts float while they sleep. Some use sleeping bags that are stuck to walls.

Life in space can be hard, but it can be fun, too!

Mae Jemison floats while she works in space

After a long day in space, Marsha Ivins goes to sleep.

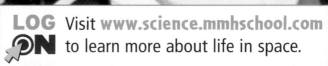

LOG ON Visit www.science.mmhschool.com to learn more about life in space.

Picture a Season

Draw a picture of your favorite season. Show what you like to do outdoors. Be sure your picture shows

● what the weather is like.

● how you are dressed.

Write a sentence to tell why the weather is like it is.

Space Trip

Suppose you are a space explorer. If you could visit the Moon or any of the planets, where would you go? Why? Tell what you would do. Write a story about your trip. Draw pictures of what you would see.

UNIT E

Exploring Indiana

LOOK!

Iron ore is melted in the high heat of a blast furnace. When the liquid metal cools and hardens it is called pig iron. This can be made into steel.

Exploring Indiana

The Power of Moving Water

A grist mill grinds wheat, rye, oat, or barley grains into flour. Many grist mills are powered by water. A water wheel is turned by the force of moving water.

Inside the mill, water power is used to turn the stones that grind the grain. This design was more popular in the late 1800s. But some grist mills are still in use today.

ACTIVITY

■ Gently blow on the "blades" of a plastic pinwheel. Describe what happens.

■ Hold the plastic pinwheel under a gentle stream of cold water in a sink. Describe what happens.

Light in Our Lives

Light is a form of energy. During the day, light coming from the Sun reaches our part of Earth. Light has to travel a great distance to reach Earth. Light moves very fast. But it takes more than 8 minutes for light to reach Earth from the Sun.

Electric energy can be used to "make" light. When a thin piece of metal in a light bulb is heated by electricity, it glows. Light is given off.

We use the light we make in many ways. Light decorates the booths and rides in a state fair.

The light given off by a lighthouse warns ships of danger.

Neon tubes can be used as art and in advertising signs. Make a list of other ways we use light.

ACTIVITY

- Glue the end of a paper towel roll to a piece of cardboard.

- Place the roll and its stand near a window.

- Measure the length of the roll's shadow at different times during the day. What happens? Why?

Indiana Test Prep

1 Grist mills can be powered by

A light

B water

C gravity

D soap

2 In what way can we "make" light?

A by using water

B by using electricity

C by using lightning

D by using sunlight

3 Which is not a source of natural light?

A   B   C   D

A Firefly

B Sun

C Moon

D Light bulb

UNIT E

Matter and Energy

LOOK!

Have you ever seen this kind of balloon? Do you know what makes these balloons move through the air? Take a good look.

Matter and Energy

Vocabulary

matter, E6

mass, E7

property, E8

temperature, E9

solid, E12

liquid, E14

volume, E15

gas, E16

physical change, E20

chemical change, E22

Did You Ever Wonder?

How do these wind surfers use all three forms of matter? The surfboard is a solid. It floats on top of water, a liquid. Air is a gas that pushes the wind surfer forward.

INQUIRY SKILL **Communicate** how we use matter at school and home.

1 Matter All Around

Get Ready

Have you ever been to a party? Suppose you were at the party in this picture. What could you see, hear, smell, and touch?

Inquiry Skill

You **observe** when you use your senses to learn about something.

Explore Activity

How can you tell what is inside?

What to do

1 **Observe** each container without opening it.

2 Predict what is inside each one. Make a chart.

3 Open each container. Did you predict correctly?

4 FURTHER INQUIRY How did you **observe** what was inside?

How are all things alike?

All things are made of **matter**. Matter is anything that takes up space. Observe the objects in this room. They are all made of matter. You are made of matter, too.

The air in these balloons is matter.

These stuffed animals are matter.

All matter also has **mass**. Mass is how much matter is in an object. A bed has a lot of mass. A goldfish has only a little mass.

 **How is everything in this room alike?**

This boy is matter.

This metal can is matter.

The water in this tank is matter.

How can you describe matter?

You use your senses to describe matter. You can describe matter by its properties. A **property** tells you something about an object. Some properties of matter are shape, size, color, and smell. Matter can sink or float. This is also a property.

big,
soft

red,
shiny

floats

sinks

Temperature measures how warm something is. Temperature is a property of matter.

Texture tells the way something feels. Texture is another property of matter.

hot

fuzzy   smooth

 What are some other properties of this stuffed frog?

Think and Write

1. What is matter?

2. Name something that has a lot of mass. Name something that has a little mass.

3. Name three properties of matter.

LOG ON Visit **www.science.mmhschool.com** to learn more about matter.

Three States of Matter

Get Ready

Matter is everywhere! What kinds of matter do you see in this picture? Which things have the most mass? Which things have the least mass?

Inquiry Skill

You put things **in order** when you tell what is first, next, and last.

E 10

Explore Activity

How can you put matter in order?

What to do

1 Which object has the most mass? The least? Predict.

2 Compare two objects on the balance. The one that makes the pan go lower has more mass.

3 Put the objects **in order** from least mass to most mass.

4 **FURTHER INQUIRY** Use a ruler to measure each object. How else can you put the objects in order?

What is a solid?

There are three different states of matter. **Solid** is one state of matter. Like all matter, a solid takes up space and has mass. But only a solid has a shape of its own. Things made out of metal, plastic, and wood are solids.

yo-yo

in-line skate

Crayon

feather

pocket game

You can measure the shape of a solid. A ruler is a tool that measures how long, wide, or high things are. This ruler measures centimeters. Some rulers measure inches.

ruler

You can measure the mass of a solid. A balance is a tool that measures mass. The side of the balance that is lower holds the thing that has more mass.

balance

How are all of these objects alike?

What is a liquid?

Liquid is another state of matter.
A liquid takes up space and has mass.
A liquid does not have a shape of its
own. It takes the shape of its container.
Milk, juice, and water are all liquids.

oil

liquid
soap

milk

juice

Volume is the amount of space that something takes up. You can measure the volume of a liquid. A measuring cup is one way to measure volume. A measuring cup can hold the same amount of liquid every time.

▷ **How can you measure the volume of this punch?**

What is a gas?

The third state of matter is **gas**. It takes up space and has mass. Gas spreads out to fill its container. It does not have a shape of its own.

Air is made up of gases. You can not see it, but air is everywhere. It can fill up a tire or a ball.

kite

air pump
and tire

balloons

When you blow up a ball, gas fills the inside. Gas pushes out the sides and makes the ball bigger.

When a gas is heated, it spreads out. It fills more of its container. When a gas is cooled, it spreads out less. It fills less of its container.

▶ **Where is gas in each of these pictures?**

Think and Write

1. What are three states of matter?

2. What kind of matter is an ice cube?

3. What kind of matter is air?

MORE TO READ Read **Solids, Liquids, and Gases** by Louise Osborne, Deborah Hodge, and Ray Boudreau.

Changing Matter

Get Ready

Have you ever put two or more things together to make something new? Look at this work of art. How would you make something like this?

Inquiry Skill

You **investigate** when you make a plan and try it out.

Explore Activity

How can you change matter?

glue

paper

scissors

craft materials

What to do

1 Observe your objects.

2 **Investigate** how to change and put together the objects. Make a plan and try it out.

> **BE CAREFUL!** Scissors are sharp.

3 What did you make? What did you do to make it? Tell how you changed matter.

4 **FURTHER INQUIRY** **Investigate** how water can change matter. What happens when you wet your object?

What is physical change?

Matter may change in different ways. You can change the size or shape of matter. This is called a **physical change**.

In a physical change, you can cut, fold, bend, or tear matter. When you only change the shape of matter, its mass stays the same.

You can also change matter by mixing it. A mixture is made of two or more different things. You can mix solids, liquids, and gases. You can separate them from a mixture too.

Mixing is a physical change. When pieces of matter are mixed together, each piece is the same as it was before it was mixed.

The salad and salad dressing are both mixtures.

▶ **Which has more mass, a head of lettuce, or a head of lettuce torn into pieces?**

What is chemical change?

Sometimes matter can change into different matter. This is called a **chemical change**. When matter goes through a chemical change, its properties change.

Burning is a chemical change. It changes wood to ashes.

Rusting is a chemical change. Some metals can rust.

Baking is a chemical change. You can heat flour, milk, sugar, and eggs to make bread.

All matter does not change in the same way. The air can change the color of a fruit. An apple will turn brown. Water and air can cause iron to rust. They can not cause plastic to change.

Before	After

▶ **What happens when something goes through a chemical change?**

Think and Write

1. Name a physical change.

2. What is a mixture?

3. Name a chemical change.

LOG ON Visit www.science.mmhschool.com to learn more about how matter can change.

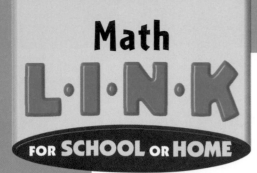
Take a Closer Look

Some objects are made of small parts. Scientists use microscopes and hand lenses to observe them. You can use two hand lenses to look at objects. Hold one hand lens above the other one and observe.

Try This!

Practice using hand lenses. Observe cloth, hair, or paper. Then use hand lenses to observe seeds inside fruits. How many seeds do you see? Record the numbers in a bar graph.

Write a Secret Note

Dip a cotton swab into a glass of milk or lemon juice. Write a message on white paper with the cotton swab. Let the note dry. Then hold the note up to a window on a sunny day. Watch to see what happens!

Try This!

Writing That Explains Write a letter to a friend. Explain how to write a secret note. Ask your friend to tell you what happens.

Vocabulary

chemical
change, E22

gas, E16

liquid, E14

mass, E7

matter, E6

physical
change, E20

property, E8

solid, E12

temperature,
E9

volume, E15

Use each word once for items 1–9.

1 Anything that takes up space and has mass is ____ .

2 The amount of matter in an object is called its ____ .

3 The size, shape, or color of an object is a ____ of the object.

4 Matter that has a shape of its own is called a ____ .

5 Matter, such as juice, that has no shape of its own is called a ____ .

6 The amount of space something takes up is called its ____ .

7 Matter, such as air, that spreads out to fill its container is called a ____ .

8 The ____ is a measure of how hot something is.

9 Write which type of change each picture shows.

A

B

Science Ideas

Tell what kind of matter each picture shows.

10

11

12

Inquiry Skill: Investigate

13 Write a plan for how you could change this clay by making only physical changes.

Did You Ever
Wonder?

INQUIRY SKILL **Investigate** why chemical changes are important. What chemical changes happen when people cook?

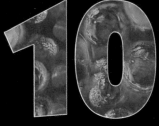

CHAPTER

10 Energy

Vocabulary

energy, E32

heat, E32

fuel, E34

light, E38

reflect, E38

refraction, E39

sound, E44

vibrate, E44

pitch, E47

Did You Ever Wonder?

What happens when fireworks explode? They make sound, light, and heat. These are all forms of energy.

INQUIRY SKILL Classify things at home or school that make sound, light, or heat.

E 29

Heat

Get Ready

A cold treat is great on a hot day. But the treat won't last long. Look at the picture. What do you think makes this ice cream lose its shape? Tell your ideas to a partner.

Inquiry Skill

You **communicate** when you share your ideas with others.

Explore Activity

How can heat change matter?

What to do

1 Find a sunny spot. Place the ice cube, butter, and chocolate on the plates. Draw how they look.

2 How will the Sun change each item? Leave the paper plates in the Sun.

3 **Communicate** what happens to each item. Draw how they look. Compare your pictures.

4 **FURTHER INQUIRY** How did heat change matter? **Communicate** your ideas to a partner.

What you need

paper plates

ice cube

butter

chocolate

How can heat change matter?

Energy can make matter move or change. One kind of energy is **heat**. Heat can change matter from one state to another. Taking away heat can change a liquid to a solid. Adding heat can change a liquid to a gas. These changes are physical changes.

Water takes the shape of its container.

The tray is put in the freezer. The liquid will change to a solid state. The plastic tray will not change.

The solid ice cubes are placed in a pan and left at room temperature.

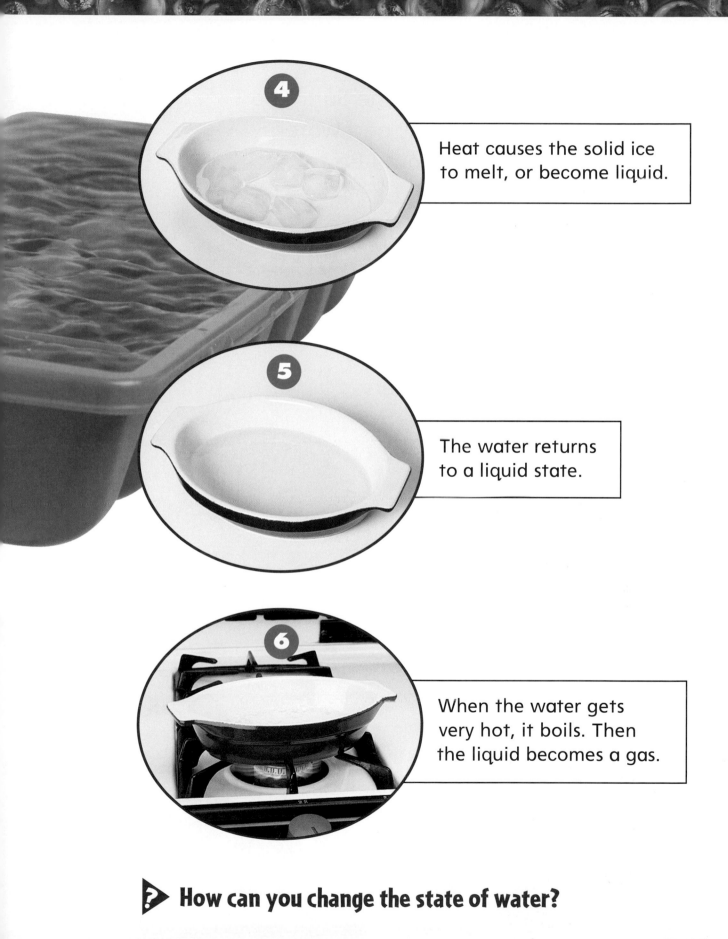

4 Heat causes the solid ice to melt, or become liquid.

5 The water returns to a liquid state.

6 When the water gets very hot, it boils. Then the liquid becomes a gas.

▶ **How can you change the state of water?**

How can we use heat?

Much of our heat is from the Sun. The Sun warms Earth's land, air, and water. Without the Sun, Earth would be too cold for things to live.

Fire gives off heat. To do this, it burns **fuel**. Wood, natural gas, and oil are fuels.

Heat can come from electricity, too. We can use dams on rivers to make electricity.

You can rub your hands to make heat. Then you can hold a pencil. The heat moves from your hand to the pencil. Heat can move from one object to another. Heat moves through metal quickly. That is why people use metal pans when they cook.

Heat can change things. When a potter puts clay in a special oven, it changes. It becomes very hard.

▶ **How is heat used in these pictures?**

Think and Write

1. Name two ways heat can change matter.

2. Where does much of our heat come from?

HOME ACTIVITY Put a tray of water and a wooden block in the freezer for two hours. What happens to each one?

Light

Look at the buildings in this picture. What do you see? What direction is the light coming from?

Inquiry Skill

You **observe** when you use your senses to find out about something.

Explore Activity

How does light move?

What you need

flashlight

mirror

What to do

1 Stand near a wall with the flashlight. Have a partner hold the mirror.

2 Shine the flashlight at the mirror. Your partner will use the mirror to aim the light on the wall.

3 **Observe** what happens to the light. How does light move?

4 FURTHER INQUIRY Shine the flashlight on other objects. **Observe** how light moves.

What is light?

Light is a kind of energy that lets us see. Light travels in straight lines.

When light hits an object, some of it **reflects**, or bounces off, the object. When light reflects off smooth, flat objects like mirrors, it bounces in one direction.

This mirror is not flat. When light hits the surface, it bounces off in many directions. This makes your reflection look funny.

When an object blocks light, it makes a shadow. A shadow is a dark area that light does not reach. You can make a shadow on the wall by blocking light with your hand. Some objects do not block light. They do not make shadows.

Glass or water can bend light. This is called **refraction**. A hand lens bends light. Bending light can make something look bigger.

How does light travel?

Light bends when it travels through this hand lens. Bent light makes the butterfly look bigger.

How do we use light?

Much of Earth's light is from the Sun. Living things need the energy from sunlight. Without the Sun, Earth would be in darkness. Nothing would be able to live or grow here.

People once used fire for light indoors and at night. Now we use electric lights to help us see.

▶ **How is light being used in these pictures?**

Think and Write

1. What is light?

2. How is a shadow made?

3. What gives us light energy after dark?

LOG ON Visit www.science.mmhschool.com to learn more about light.

6 Sound

Get Ready

Sounds are all around us. Look closely at this picture. How are these people making sound? What do you think it sounds like?

Inquiry Skill

You **observe** when you use your senses to find out about something.

Explore Activity

How is sound made?

What you need

paper cup

string

goggles

paper clip

What to do

1 Work with two partners. Make a tiny hole in the bottom of the cup. Tie the string to the paper clip. Pull the string through the hole.

2 Hold the cup and string with one partner. The other partner snaps the string. **BE CAREFUL!** Wear goggles.

3 **Observe** what happens. How did you make sound?

4 **FURTHER INQUIRY** Change the length of the string. **Observe** what happens. How does the sound change?

E 43

What is sound?

Sound is a kind of energy. Sound is made when something **vibrates**, or moves back and forth. When something vibrates it makes the air around it vibrate, too. Vibrating air moves to your ear. It makes part of your ear vibrate. That is how you hear.

When you speak, air from your lungs makes your vocal cords vibrate. Touch your throat as you speak. Feel the vibration.

Sound travels in waves. Sound waves move through the air like ripples in a pond.

▶ **What carries most of the sound you hear?**

What makes loud and soft sounds?

Not all sounds are the same. Some sounds are loud. Big vibrations make loud sounds. Some sounds are soft. Small vibrations make soft sounds. The farther away you are from a sound, the softer it sounds to you.

▷ **How would you compare the sound of a motorcycle to the sound of a bicycle?**

What is pitch?

Sounds can also be high, low, or somewhere in between. **Pitch** is how high or how low a sound is.

Musical instruments work by vibrating. Look at this instrument. When you hit a small bar, the vibrations are fast. The pitch is high. When you hit a big bar, the vibrations are slow. The pitch is low.

high pitch

low pitch

? **How would you describe the pitch of each dog's bark?**

What can sound move through?

Sound can move through gases, liquids, and solids. Most sound you hear is moving through air. Air is made of gases.

You can hear sounds underwater. Sounds move differently through water and air. The sounds make the water vibrate.

Have you put your ear to a desk or a door and heard a sound from the other side? The sound makes the wood vibrate. The wood is a solid.

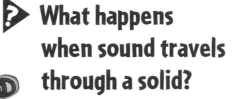

What happens when sound travels through a solid?

Think and Write

1. How is sound made?

2. What is pitch?

3. Tell what sound can move through.

MORE TO READ

Read **Energy** by Alvin Silverstein, Virginia Silverstein, and Laura Silverstein Nunn.

Thomas Alva Edison

by Tamera Bryant
illustrated by Laurie Jordan

McGraw Hill

Write About the Past

Think about what life was like before electric light bulbs. Read *Thomas Alva Edison* by Tamera Bryant. Think about all the things that Edison invented. How did they change people's lives?

Try This!

How would your life be different without Thomas Edison's inventions? Write a story about what your life might have been like.

Make Your Own Music

People have been making music for a very long time. The first instruments invented were probably hollow logs used as drums. You can invent your own instrument, too.

Try This!

Think of ways to make a musical instrument. Find things that can make sounds. Try to make sounds with high pitch and low pitch. Can you play a tune?

Science Newsroom CD-ROM Choose **Bouncing Sounds** to learn more about sound.

Chapter 10 Review

Vocabulary

energy, E32

fuel, E34

heat, E32

light, E38

pitch, E47

reflects, E38

refraction, E39

sound, E44

vibrates, E44

Use each word once for items 1–9.

1 When you make matter move or change you use ____ .

2 Energy that can change the state of matter is called ____ .

3 Something that gives off heat when it burns is ____ .

4 Energy that you hear is called ____ .

5 How high or low a sound is, is called its ____ .

6 When something moves back and forth quickly, it ____ .

7 Energy that allows you to see is called ____ .

8 When light bounces off a mirror, the mirror ____ the light.

9 When something bends light, it is called ____ .

Science Ideas

10 What can sound move through?

11 Which picture shows heat?

A

B

C

Inquiry Skill: Communicate

Tell what each of these pictures shows.

12

13

READ

Fossil Fuels Keep Us Warm by Shirley Granahan

Sending a Message with Dots...and Dashes... by Emily North

Did You Ever Wonder?

[INQUIRY SKILL] **Investigate** loud and quiet sounds at school or home. How can loud sounds be helpful?

A GLOW-ING IDEA!

When Becky Schroeder was ten years old, she had a really bright idea. One afternoon, she was doing homework while in the car with her mom. Soon it got dark. Becky wanted to see what she was writing without turning on a light. So she invented a way to do it.

Becky Schroeder
has dreamed up
nine inventions....
This is one of
them.

Becky Schroeder's Glo-sheet

Becky and her dad bought special paint that glowed after light hit it. Becky coated a clipboard with the paint and took the clipboard into a dark room. The board glowed . . . even through the piece of paper she had placed on top! Now she could write in the dark. Becky named her invention the Glo-sheet.

Young inventor Becky Schroeder

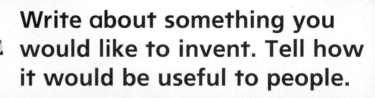

Write about something you would like to invent. Tell how it would be useful to people.

Matter, Matter Everywhere

Look at the object. What state of matter is the object? What are its properties? How can you make a physical change to it? How can you make a chemical change to it? Make a book to show your ideas.

Heat, Sound, and Light

Think of three objects that give off heat, sound, or light. Draw a picture of each. Then create an invention that uses heat, sound, or light. Write or tell what your invention does. How can it help people?

UNIT F

Exploring Indiana

Take a good look. This roller coaster car has no motor. After the roller coaster reaches the top of the first hill, gravity keeps the cars moving—and moving fast!

Exploring Indiana

Machines in Action

It takes many parts to make a machine like a car or truck. With machines we can lift and move heavy objects.

This ramp is a simple machine. It makes getting the heavy cartons onto the truck easier. How does it work?

New cars are loaded onto a truck for transport. They may travel from Indiana to other parts of the country without being driven. This way, the cars are still new.

What DO YOU THINK?

The man in the photograph is moving a box. What machine is he using? Could the same machine also be used to do other work? Discuss your ideas.

Finding Your Way

There are many hiking trails in Indiana. Hikers carry backpacks and go for long walks along these trails.

Hikers must be careful not to get lost. What would a hiker do if there were no signs marking the path? There are a number of different tools hikers can use to tell where they are.

How can you be sure you are walking in the right direction? Hikers use a compass. Because the compass needle always points north, you can easily read the other direction points on a compass.

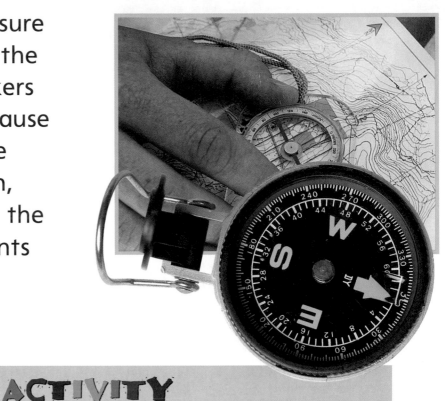

ACTIVITY

Make a Map of Your Classroom

- Stand in the middle of your classroom. Use a compass to find out which direction is north.

- Write N, S, E, W on four pieces of paper. Place them at the sides of the room to tell you which direction you are facing.

- Draw a map of the classroom.

- Use your map to tell:

    - Which side of the classroom has the teacher's desk?

    - If you wanted to walk from your desk to the door, which direction would you walk?

Indiana Test Prep

1 What does a ramp help us do?

   A tell time

   B lift and move heavy objects

   C travel to space

   D learn information

2 What do hikers use to tell the direction in which they are walking?

   A a ramp

   B a compass

   C a car

   D a truck

3 Which object would you use to move a heavy load onto a platform four feet above the floor?

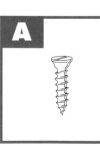 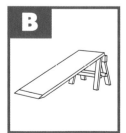  

UNIT

F Watch It Move

Watch It Move

LOOK!

Snowboarding is like skateboarding without wheels! How does this snowboarder move forward? Take a good look.

11 Forces and Machines

Did You Ever Wonder?

What makes things move? Pushes and pulls do. The parts of this machine move because of pushes and pulls. What are some machines that use pushes and pulls?

 **INQUIRY SKILL** **Observe** how you use pushes and pulls every day.

Vocabulary

force, F6

gravity, F7

friction, F12

simple machine, F20

lever, F21

fulcrum, F21

ramp, F26

F 3

Pushes and Pulls

Get Ready

Have you ever played with marbles? They can move far if you give them a push. How far can a marble move?

Inquiry Skill

You **measure** when you find out how far something moves.

Explore Activity

How far can different things move?

What to do

1 Line up objects at a starting line.

2 Tap each object to move it forward. Do not tap one harder than the others.

3 **Measure** how far each object moved. Use a ruler. Record the numbers. Which object moved the farthest? Why?

4 ☐ FURTHER INQUIRY ☐ Tap the objects harder than before. **Measure** how far they moved.

What you need

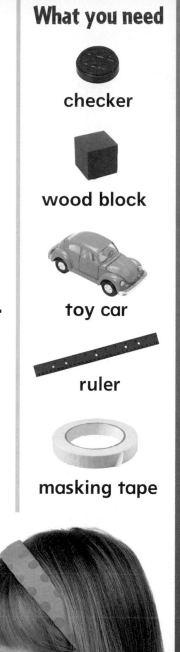

checker

wood block

toy car

ruler

masking tape

What makes things move?

Things can not move on their own. A push or a pull makes something move or change direction. A push or a pull is called a **force**.

When the man pulls the sled, he uses force to move it. When the adults push the girl, they use force to move her.

pull

push

Gravity is a force that pulls things toward Earth. When you go downhill, gravity makes you speed up. It also holds you back when you go uphill.

Gravity holds you on Earth. You can see the pull of gravity when you let go of an object. It falls toward Earth.

▷ **What are some forces that make things move?**

Gravity pulls things downhill.

How do objects move?

Objects can move in different ways. You can tell how objects move by the paths they make.

The roller coaster ride begins in a straight line. But soon it moves on a curved path. The swing ride moves in a circle.

circle

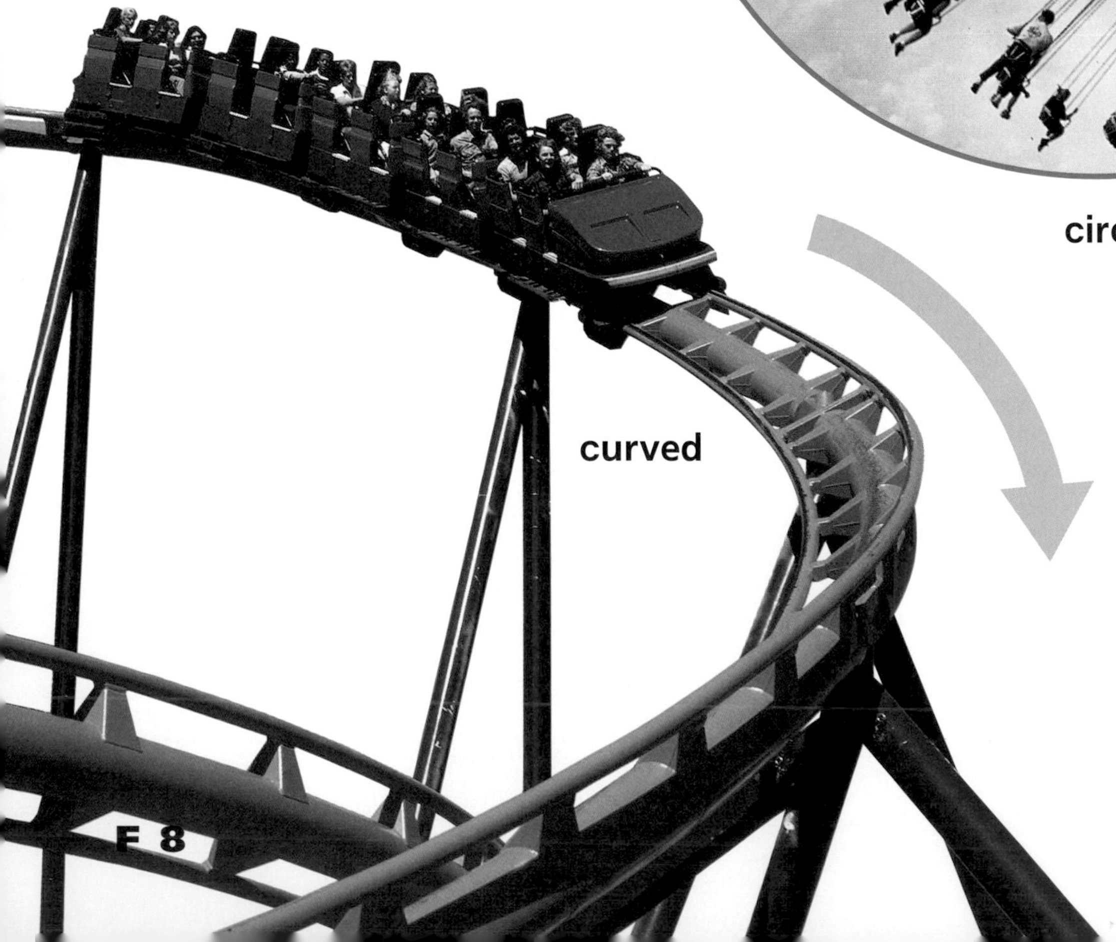

curved

This ride moves back and forth. Some things, like the ball below, move in a zigzag. A zigzag is a path with short, sharp turns from one side to another.

back and forth

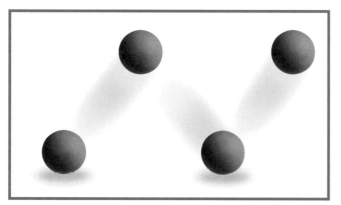

zigzag

 What makes these things move?

Think and Write

1. How can you make something move?

2. What is gravity?

3. What are some ways objects can move?

HOME ACTIVITY Look around your home. Make a list of how things that you see move.

Forces and Change

Get Ready

Do you think this truck could go faster here or on a street? Why?

Inquiry Skill

You **compare** when you tell how things are alike and different.

Explore Activity

How can you slow down a force?

What to do

1 Stack the books. Put the edge of the board on the books to make a hill.

2 Put the bus at the top of the hill and let go. Do not push it. Place tape where the bus stopped.

3 Cover the board with wax paper. Repeat step 2. Try the activity again with sandpaper, then cloth.

4 FURTHER INQUIRY
Compare how far the bus went each time. What slowed down the bus most? Why?

What you need

cardboard

3 books

toy bus

wax paper

sandpaper

cloth

tape

What slows things down?

Friction is a force that slows down moving things. It happens when two things rub together.

There is more friction between rough surfaces than between smooth ones. It is harder to push or pull something over a rough surface than over a smooth surface.

When you skate, your wheels move along a surface. To stop, you drag a rubber stopper on the ground. You will slow down until you stop. This happens because dragging causes friction.

What force slows down the cart? The skater?

What happens when you change a force?

When a force changes, the way a thing moves changes, too. A little force can make a golf ball move slowly. More force can make the golf ball move faster and farther.

It takes more force to move some things than it does to move others. The heavier something is, the more force you need to move it.

Who is using more force to pull the luggage?

How can force change motion?

When something moves, it is in motion. A force can make something in motion stop. A force can make something standing still start to move. These are changes in motion. Forces make these changes happen.

Forces can change the motion of things. They can make things speed up, slow down, stop, and start moving. They can make things change direction, too.

The pushing force of the bowling ball changes the motion of the pins.

In a game of table tennis, you use a paddle to hit the ball across the net. Each hit is a push. The push changes the direction of the ball.

▶ **How does the motion of the ball change when you play table tennis?**

table tennis

Think and Write

1. What is friction?

2. What can happen to an object when the force on it gets stronger?

3. What are some changes in motion?

 **MORE TO READ**   Read **Push and Pull (The Way Things Move)** by Lola M. Schaefer and Gail Saunders-Smith.

Levers

Get Ready

This circus boy wants to move the stand. How can he use force to move it? He's got a plan. Can you guess what it is?

Inquiry Skill

You **investigate** when you make a plan and try it out.

Explore Activity

How can force help you lift things?

What you need

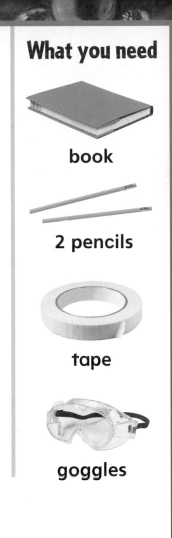

book

2 pencils

tape

goggles

What to do

1 Tape a pencil to your desk. Place the book next to the pencil.

2 Look at the pictures below. Predict which is the easiest way to lift the book.

3 Make a plan. Then try it out.

BE CAREFUL! Wear goggles.

4 **FURTHER INQUIRY** **Investigate** how to lift other objects in the same way.

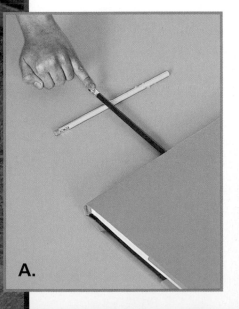

A.

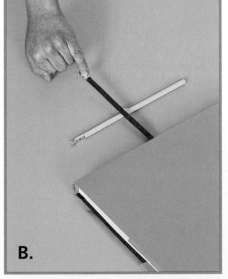

B.

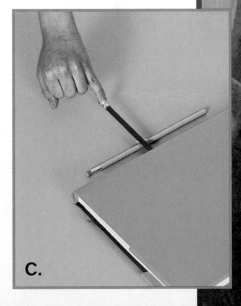

C.

What is a simple machine?

A **simple machine** makes moving an object easier. A simple machine uses force to move the object, or load, from one place to another.

You need to use a lot of force to move a heavy object. When you use a simple machine, it is easier to move the same object.

▷ **How do you know the seesaw is a simple machine?**

What is a lever?

A **lever** is a simple machine. A lever is a bar that rests on a **fulcrum**, or fixed point. A lever may look like a seesaw.

To use a lever, you put a load on one side of the bar. When you put force on the other side, the load is lifted.

▶ **Where is the fulcrum on this lever?**

How a lever works

force

load

fulcrum

lift

How do we use levers?

You can find levers in many tools. A hand truck is a lever. The fulcrum is the wheel. A pair of scissors is a lever, too. The fulcrum is the point where the blades cross.

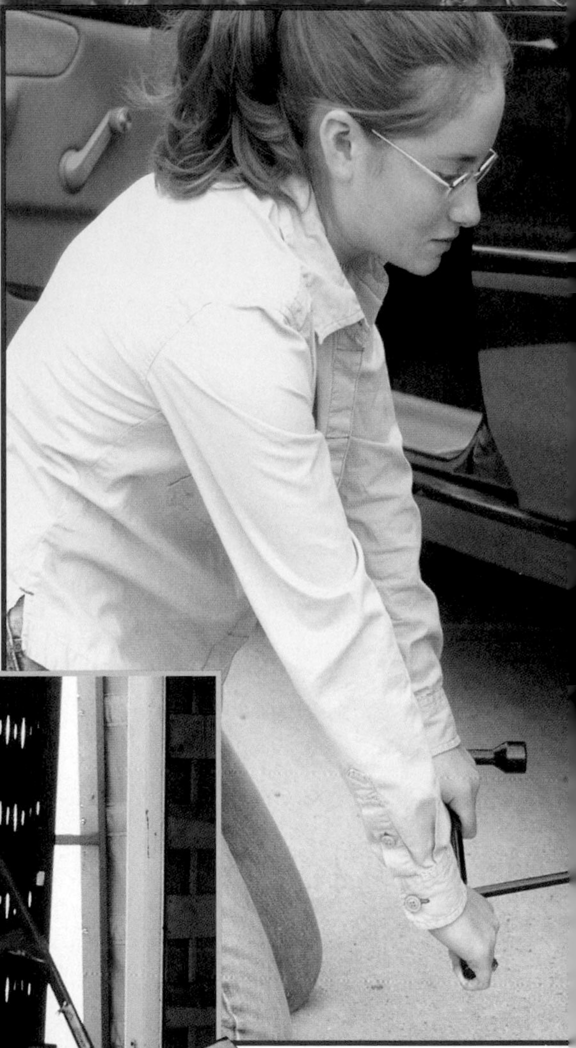

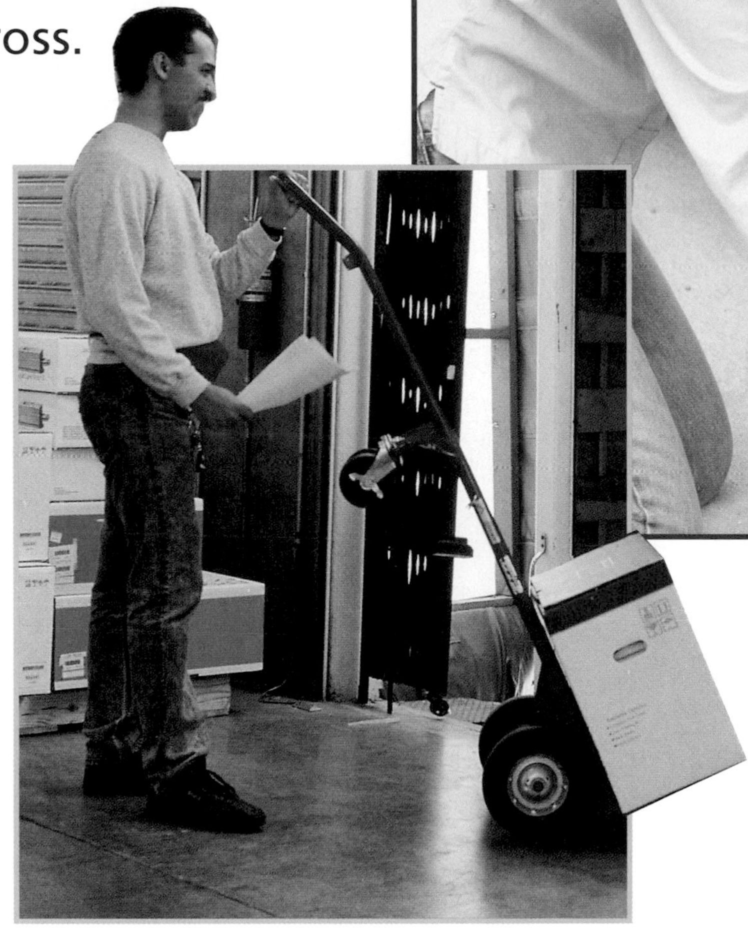

hand truck

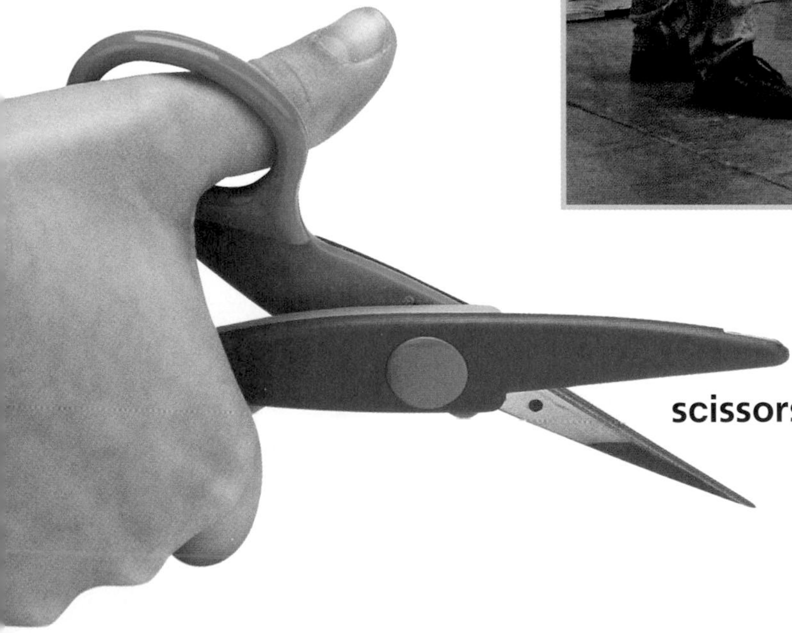

scissors

A car jack is a lever. With a car jack, you can lift a car. A crowbar is a lever, too. You can use it to pry things apart.

▶ How can levers help us do work?

crowbar

car jack

Think and Write

1. Why do we use simple machines?

2. Name one kind of simple machine.

3. What tools use levers?

HOME ACTIVITY List any levers you find in your home.

4 Ramps

Get Ready

How do you think these pyramids were built? The blocks are too large to lift. What tool did people use to move the blocks?

Inquiry Skill

You **measure** something when you find out how much of it there is.

Explore Activity

How can you use less force to move things?

What you need

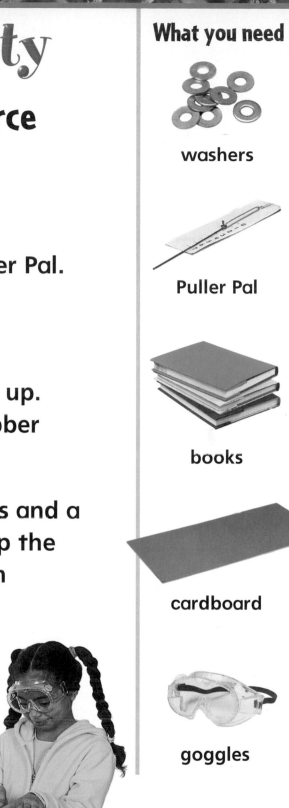

washers

Puller Pal

books

cardboard

goggles

What to do

1 Tie 10 washers to the Puller Pal. This tool measures force.

BE CAREFUL! Wear goggles.

2 Lift the Puller Pal straight up. **Measure** how far the rubber band stretches.

3 Make a ramp out of books and a board. Pull the washers up the board and measure. When did you use less force?

4 FURTHER INQUIRY

Take away some books from your ramp. **Measure** and compare how much force you used.

How does a ramp work?

A **ramp** is a simple machine with a slanted surface. A ramp can help you move things to a higher place. It takes a lot of force to lift a load. It takes less force to push a load up a ramp.

A ramp can be short and steep.
Or it can be longer and less steep.
It takes more force to push something
up a steep ramp than up one that is
longer and less steep.

 **What can you use to move a heavy load?**

How do we use ramps?

Ramps help people move objects from one place to another. Many buildings have ramps as well as stairs. They make it easier for people to move from floor to floor.

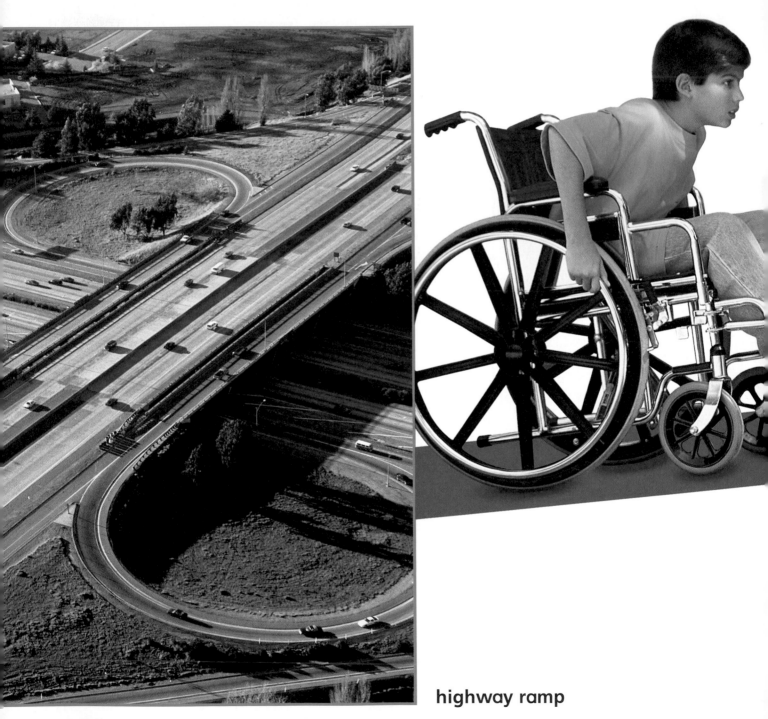

highway ramp

Some ramps are for cars and trucks. Ramps make it possible for these heavy machines to move to high places.

 How are people in these pictures using ramps?

boat ramp

loading ramp

wheelchair ramp

Think and Write

1. What is a ramp?

2. Why is it easier to move something up a ramp than it is to lift it?

3. Name two ways people use ramps.

LOG ON Visit **www.science.mmhschool.com** to find out more about forces and machines.

Make a Book of Forces

You use pushes and pulls all day long. Find out what everyday activities use force. Read *When Zeke Is Home Alone* by Linda Cernak.

I went down the slide today.

Try This!

Draw pictures of a few ways you use forces during the day. Write a sentence about each. Put your pictures into a book.

Science Newsroom CD-ROM Choose **Gravity** to solve problems about gravity.

Join the Fun Force!

Think about the many different ways you can move. Can you walk in a zigzag line or in a curved line? Can you walk in a straight line or in circles?

Try This!

Writing About Yourself Think about a time when you played Follow the Leader. How did the leader tell you to move? Write a letter to a friend. Tell how you moved to play the game.

Chapter 11 Review

Vocabulary

force, F6

friction, F12

fulcrum, F21

gravity, F7

lever, F21

simple machines, F20

ramp, F26

Use each word once for items 1–7.

1 A push or a pull on an object is a ____ .

2 The force that pulls things toward Earth is ____ .

3 The force that slows down a moving object is ____ .

4 A ramp and a lever are ____ .

What is the arrow pointing to?

Science Ideas

8 Which picture does not show a lever?

A

B

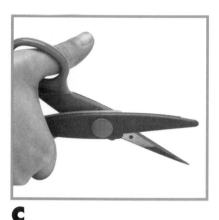

C

Inquiry Skill: Measure

9 Which takes more force to move along a ramp, a ruler or a box of crayons? Use the Puller Pal to find out. Measure how far the rubber band stretches.

READ
Levers and Ramps by Susan Rogers

Did You Ever Wonder?

INQUIRY SKILL
Use blocks to **make a model** of a ramp.

Forces and Magnets

Vocabulary

attract, F38

pole, F40

repel, F41

magnetic field, F42

compass, F49

Did You Ever Wonder?

What part of a magnet is the strongest?
Magnets are strongest at the ends!
What kinds of things stick to magnets?

INQUIRY SKILL **Observe** how magnets
help people. Why are magnets useful?

All About Magnets

Get Ready

How do these pins stick without glue? What is holding them on the magnet? In what ways are the pins all alike?

Inquiry Skill

You **classify** when you look at how things are alike to put them into groups.

Explore Activity

What will stick to a magnet?

What to do

1 Make a magnet fishing pole. Tie string to a pencil. Tie a magnet to the end of the string.

2 Put all the objects in a bag. Predict which objects will stick to the magnet.

3 Use the fishing pole to fish out objects from the bag.

4 FURTHER INQUIRY Classify each object to show whether it sticks to the magnet. List the objects on a chart.

Sticks	Does Not Stick

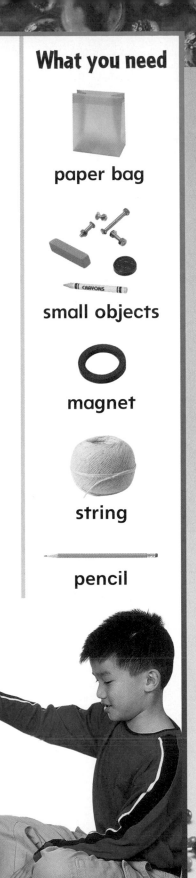

paper bag

small objects

magnet

string

pencil

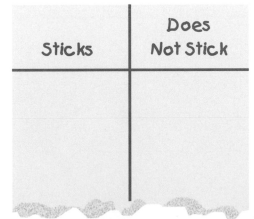

What does a magnet pull?

A magnet can push and pull. This is called magnetic force.

A magnet can **attract**, or pull, some metals. It attracts metals made of iron. A magnet will not attract things made of copper, brass, plastic, wood, or rubber.

Magnets may have different sizes and shapes. A magnet can be in the shape of a bar, circle, or horseshoe.

Different magnets may also have different pushing and pulling strengths.

▶ **Tell which objects a magnet can attract.**

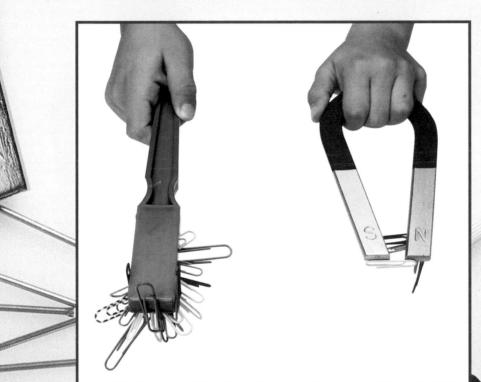

What are poles?

Magnets have two **poles**. The poles are where the pull of the magnet is strongest. Each magnet has a north pole and a south pole.

Look at the picture below. These magnetic poles attract each other. This is because they are opposites. A north pole and a south pole pull toward each other.

Now look at this picture. The poles of these magnets **repel**, or push away from, each other. They are repelling each other because they are the same. Two poles that are the same push each other away.

 What would happen if you tried to put two south poles together?

What can magnets pull through?

Magnets can attract objects without even touching them. A magnet can pull through solids, liquids, and gases. The area around a magnet where its force pulls is called a **magnetic field**.

Magnets can pull through liquids.

Magnets can pull through solids.

A magnet's force is strongest when the magnet is close to an iron object. The force grows weaker as the magnet is moved away. When a magnet is moved far enough away from the object, it will not attract the object.

▷ **What are the magnets pulling through in these pictures?**

Think and Write

1. What kinds of objects can magnets attract?

2. What is a magnetic field?

3. Tell what magnets can pull through.

 **MORE TO READ**

Read **Magnetism and Magnets** by Michael Flaherty.

Everyday Magnets

Get Ready

Look at the picture. What are these kinds of magnets used for? How do they work? If you could make your own magnet, what would you use it for?

Inquiry Skill

You **communicate** when you share your ideas with others.

Explore Activity

How can you make a magnet?

What you need

nail

bar magnet

paper clips

What to do

1 Rub the nail in one direction against the magnet. Do this 50 times or more. **BE CAREFUL!** Nails are sharp.

2 How many paper clips can your nail pick up? **Communicate** what happens.

3 What else can your nail pick up? Make a list.

4 **FURTHER INQUIRY** Rub the nail 20 times. How many paper clips can your nail pick up? **Communicate** what happens.

can opener

How do we use magnets every day?

You can use a magnet to pick up things or to hold things together. At home, magnets keep your cupboard door closed. Magnets also can lift the top off a can.

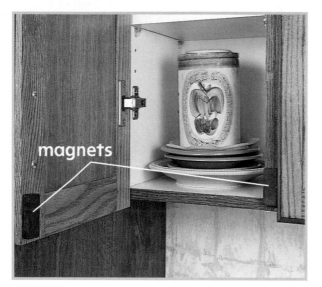

magnets

cupboard door

screwdriver

ITALIAN STYLE
PEELED TOMATOES

Many tools have magnets in them. These tools can make it easier to pick up nails, screws, and bolts.

Some special magnets can help with big jobs. This giant magnet can lift heavy junk from the trash pile.

 How are these magnets being used?

How is Earth like a magnet?

Did you know that Earth is like a giant magnet? It has a North Pole and a South Pole. Earth's magnetic field stretches out into space. Like all magnets, Earth's pulling force is strongest at its poles.

North Pole

South Pole

People use Earth's magnetic field to help them find their way. A **compass** is a tool with a magnetic needle that always points to Earth's North Pole. With a compass, you can always figure out which direction you are facing.

▶ **Where does a compass needle always point?**

Think and Write

1. What are some ways we use magnets?

2. Where is Earth's magnetic field the strongest?

3. What is a compass?

HOME ACTIVITY
Go on a magnet hunt at home. List each magnet you find. Tell how it is used.

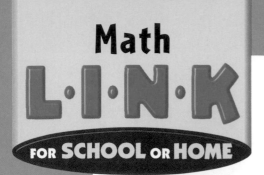

Test a Magnet's Strength

Some magnets are stronger than others. You can compare their strengths. How many objects does each magnet attract?

Magnet Strength

Number of Paper Clips

8
7
6
5
4
3
2
1
0

Kind of Magnet

Try This!

Hang a line of paper clips from different magnets until no more will hang on. Count how many clips each magnet holds. Record the numbers on a bar graph.

Make Your Own Compass

Many people use compasses to help them find their way. You can, too.

Try This!

Have an adult help you make your own magnet like you did in the Explore Activity. Magnetize a large, straightened paper clip. Stick the paper clip through a foam ball or a cork. Float it in a big bowl of water. Wait until it stops moving. Which way is north?

Vocabulary

attract, F38

compass, F49

magnetic field, F42

poles, F40

repel, F41

Use each word once for items 1–5.

1 The strongest parts of a magnet are its _____ .

2 The area around a magnet where the force pulls is called a _____ .

3 Opposite poles of a magnet pull, or _____ .

4 The same poles of two magnets _____ each other.

5 A tool with a magnetic needle that always points to Earth's North Pole is a _____ .

Science Ideas

6 Which of the following will a magnet pick up?

A

B

C

7 Find out which magnet below holds the most pieces of paper to a refrigerator. Make a plan. Get what you need to test your plan. Then try it out.

READ
Ride a Floating Train by Richie Chevat

Did You Ever Wonder? **INQUIRY SKILL** Find magnets around your home. Which is the strongest? Which is the weakest? Put the magnets **in order**.

Fred Jeffers

Magnet Physicist

Fred Jeffers has loved magnets since he was five years old. Today, Fred works with magnets that go inside computers.

You write information down on paper. A computer writes down information, too. But it does not use paper. It uses a disk. A computer saves information on a disk. The disk has a magnetic covering. Fred experiments with magnetic coverings. He looks for ways to make them better.

How can people make computers save information faster? How can disks save more information? Magnets help Fred find answers to these questions.

LOG ON Visit **www.science.mmhschool.com** to learn more about magnets.

TIME FOR KIDS

This disk is a part of a computer. It saves information.

Think Big!

How do magnets make your life better?

F 55

Forces in Sports

Choose a sport that you like. Draw a picture of you or a friend playing it. Write or tell how you use each of these things while playing:

- push or pull
- gravity
- friction

Magnet Hunt

Go on a magnet hunt around your home or school. Choose one magnet and write about it. How is the magnet used? What does it attract? How strong is its pulling force? How can you test it out?

For Your Reference

Skills Handbook

Science Handbook

Health Handbook

Glossary

Observe

You **observe** when you use your senses to learn about something. Your senses tell you how things look, sound, feel, smell, or taste.

What to do

1 Observe something in the Science Center. How does it look? Feel? Smell? Sound?

2 Draw and write about it.

3 Tell a friend which of your senses helped you the most.

pencil

crayons

paper

Inquiry Skill Builder 2

Measure

You can **measure** to find out how long, fast, or warm something is. You use numbers to record the answer.

What to do

1 Fill one cup with warm water. Fill the other cup with cold water.

2 Place a thermometer in each cup. Wait 2 minutes. **Measure** the temperatures.

3 Compare your temperatures with a partner's. Did you both get the same numbers? If not, measure again.

What you need

warm and cold water

2 thermometers

</>
Inquiry Skill Builder 3

Compare

You **compare** things when you show how they are alike and different.

What to do

1 **Compare** the people.

2 List three ways they are alike. List three ways they are different.

3 Choose an animal. How are the people different from the animal?

What you need

paper

pencil

Inquiry Skill Builder 4

Classify

You **classify** when you put things into groups to show how they are alike.

What you need

paper

pencil

What to do

1 Look at the picture of the beans.

2 Classify the beans by size. How many are big? How many are small?

3 Find another way to classify the beans.

Make a Model

You **make a model** when you do something to show a place or thing. A model can help you learn how a place looks or how a thing works.

What to do

1 Make a **model** of a clock. Include numbers and hands.

BE CAREFUL! Scissors are sharp.

2 Tell what you can learn about a real clock from the model.

3 Tell how a real clock is different from the model.

What you need

paper

crayons

scissors

paper fastener

Inquiry Skill Builder 6

Communicate

You **communicate** when you talk, write, or draw to share your ideas.

What you need

paper

pencil

What to do

1 Think about your favorite food.

2 Write about it and draw a picture.

3 **Communicate** to a friend about your favorite food. Ask your friend to name the food you described.

Infer

To **infer**, you use what you know to figure something out.

What to do

1 Look at the pictures. Record what you observe about each picture.

2 Use what you know to **infer** which place is warmer.

3 Write a short story to tell what people do to have fun in each place.

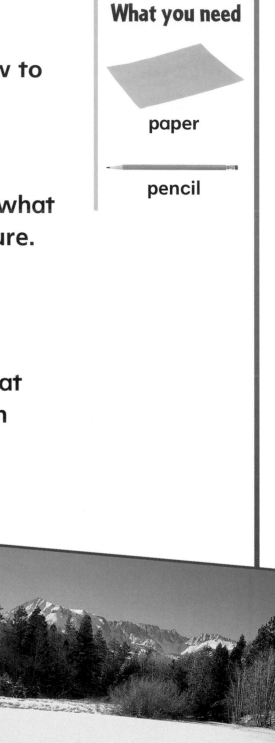

Inquiry Skill Builder 8

Put Things in Order

To put things **in order**, you tell what happens first, next, and last.

What you need

pencil

crayons

paper

What to do

1 Think about all the things that you did this morning.

2 List the things on your paper. Write them **in order**.

3 Draw a picture of you doing one of those things.

Predict

You **predict** when you use what you know to tell what you think will happen.

"I'm hungry," said Laura.

"Me, too," replied Jack.

"I wish I had a snack," Laura said.

"All I have are these grapes," said Jack.

crayons

paper

What to do

1 Read the story above.

2 **Predict** what will happen next.

3 Draw a picture to show it.

Inquiry Skill Builder 10

Investigate

When you **investigate**, you make a plan and try it out.

What to do

1 Use clay and pencils to make a shape.

2 How many blocks can your shape hold? **Investigate** to find out. Make a plan and try it.

3 Have a partner try your plan. How many blocks did your partner use? Did you use the same number?

What you need

pencils

clay

blocks

Draw a Conclusion

To **draw** a **conclusion**, you use what you observe to explain what happens.

What to do

1 Look at the picture. Where do you think the girl went? What do you think she did?

2 Draw a **conclusion**. Show it in a picture.

3 Explain your conclusion to a friend. Does your friend agree with you? Why or why not?

What you need

crayons

paper

Save and Recycle

We should not waste things.

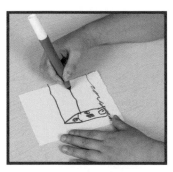

Use no more
than you need.

Don't leave
the water on.

Recycle as much
as you can.

Use things more
than once.

Care of Animals

Here are ways to care for animals.

- Give pets food and water. Give them a safe place to live, too.

- Be kind to pets. Handle them with care.

- Don't touch wild animals. They may bite, sting, or scratch you.

- Do not touch things in places where wild animals live.

Care of Plants

Here are ways to care for plants.

- Give plants water and sunlight.

- Ask the teacher before you touch or eat a plant. Some plants can make you very sick!

- Do not dig up plants or pick flowers. Let plants grow where they are.

Clean Up

We need to keep work places clean.

Let an adult clean
up broken glass.

Pour water into a sink,
not into a trash can.

Put food in plastic bags.
This keeps bugs away.

Don't get paint
or food on you.

How to Measure

You can use objects to measure. Line up the objects and count them. Use objects that are alike. They must be the same size.

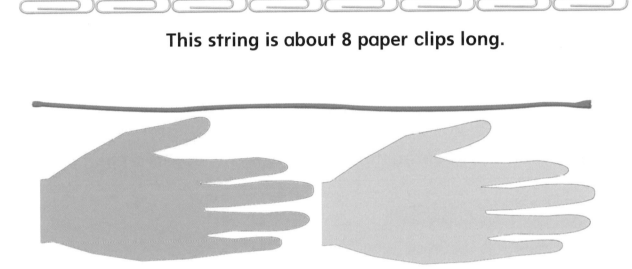

This string is about 8 paper clips long.

This string is about 2 hands long.

Try This!

● Measure some string. Tell how you did it.

● Can you measure string with these paper clips? Why or why not?

Measure in Centimeters

You can use a ruler to measure. You can use centimeters (cm). This is called a unit of measurement. You can measure this insect. Line up the end of the insect with the 0 on the ruler.

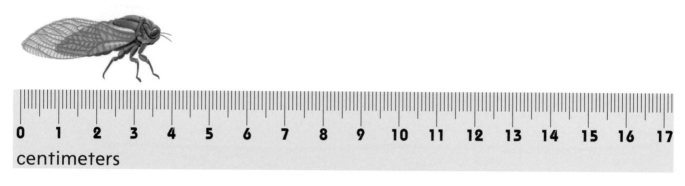

The insect is about 4 centimeters long. We write this as 4 cm.

The crayon is about $7\frac{1}{2}$ centimeters long. We write this as $7\frac{1}{2}$ cm.

Try This!

Measure this pencil. Tell how long it is.

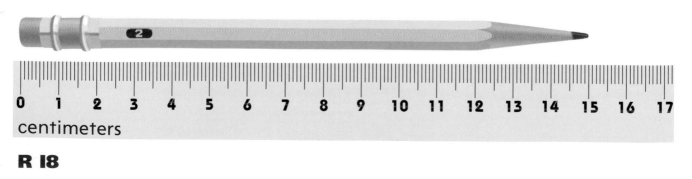

Measure in Inches

You can use inches (in.) to measure, too.
This toy is about $2\frac{1}{2}$ inches, or $2\frac{1}{2}$ in.

Inches

You can estimate how long something is.
When you estimate, you guess the length.
Then you can use a ruler to measure it.

Try This!

Estimate how long each
object is. Then use a ruler
to measure them.

Object	Estimate	Measure
penny	about ____ in.	____ in.
toy car	about ____ in.	____ in.

Use a Measuring Cup

Volume is the amount of space something takes up. You can use a measuring cup to find volume.

You can use different units to measure volume. One unit is called milliliters (mL). Another unit is called a cup. Two cups make up a pint.

Try This!

- Find a container. Estimate how much water it can hold.

- Then fill it with water. Measure the water in milliliters or cups to find out if you were right.

Use a Balance

A balance compares masses.

Place one object on each side of the balance. The object that has more mass will make that side of the balance go down. The object that has less mass will go up.

Try This!

- Place 2 objects on a balance. Which has more mass?

- Put 3 objects in order from least mass to most mass. Use the balance to check.

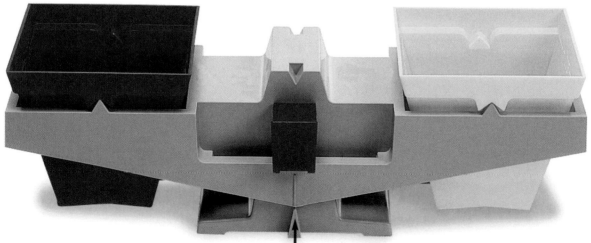

Before you compare masses, make sure the arrow points to the line.

Use a Scale

A scale measures weight. As an animal grows, it gets bigger and gains weight. You can measure weight in pounds (lbs).

Try This!

- **What is your weight? First, estimate your weight. Then, use a scale to measure it.**

- **Every month, measure your weight. Record it in a chart. See how your weight changes as you grow.**

Use a Thermometer

A thermometer measures temperature.
There is liquid inside the thermometer.

When it gets warmer, the liquid
moves up.

When it gets cooler, the liquid
moves down.

Which thermometer shows a warmer
temperature? How can you tell?

A thermometer measures temperature in degrees. The marks show degrees Fahrenheit and degrees Celsius.

Read this thermometer in degrees Celsius. Look at the numbers on the right side. Find the number where the liquid ends.

degrees
Celsius

degrees
Fahrenheit

Try This!

Read the thermometers on page R24. What temperatures are shown?

Use Weather Tools

You can use weather tools to measure the weather. A thermometer tells you how hot or cool the air is outside.

A rain gauge tells you how much rain falls. It has a jar that catches the rain. It also has a ruler to measure how much rain falls into the jar.

weather vane

rain gauge

wind sock

A wind sock and weather vane tell which way the wind blows. The arrow on a weather vane tells where the wind is coming from. It points to the north, south, east, or west.

An anemometer measures how fast the wind blows. It tells you the wind's speed.

Try This!

Use a rain gauge. Measure how much rain falls on two different days that rain. Compare the amounts.

anemometer

Use a Clock

A clock measures time.

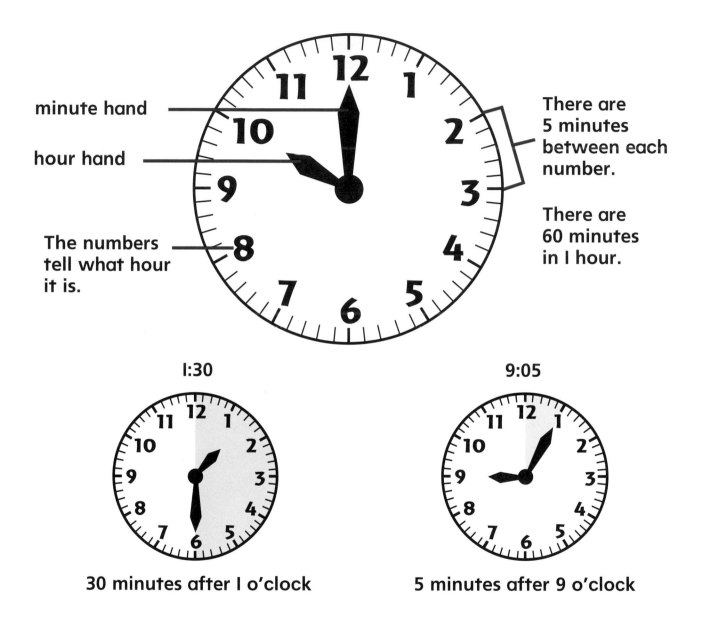

minute hand

hour hand

The numbers tell what hour it is.

There are 5 minutes between each number.

There are 60 minutes in 1 hour.

1:30

30 minutes after 1 o'clock

9:05

5 minutes after 9 o'clock

Try This!

Estimate how long you sleep each night. Use a clock to find out.

Use a Hand Lens

A hand lens makes objects seem larger.

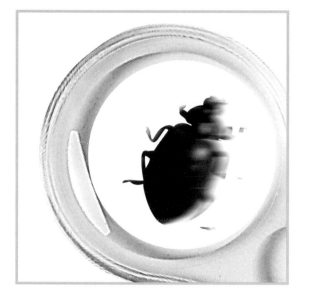

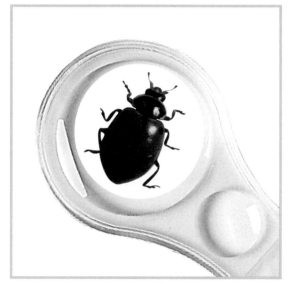

First, move the lens away from the object. Stop when the object looks fuzzy.

Next, move the lens a little closer to the object. Stop when the object looks clear.

Try This!

- Observe each bug here. Use a hand lens.

- How many legs do you see on the bugs?

- What else can you see?

Use a Computer

You can use a computer to get information.

You can use CD-ROMs. They save a lot of information. You can fit many books on one CD-ROM!

You can also use the Internet. The Internet links your computer to ones far away.

Try This!

Visit **www.science.mmhschool.com** to find out more about science in your world.

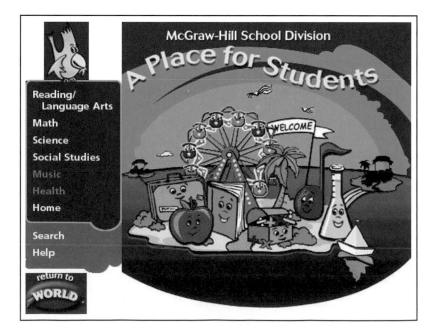

Your Body

Each part of your body has a job to do.

brain
Your brain lets you think and tells your body what to do.

lungs
Your lungs help you breathe oxygen.

heart
Your heart is a muscle that pumps blood.

bones
Your bones are hard body parts that make up your skeleton.

stomach
Your stomach changes food you eat into energy.

muscles
Your muscles help you move through pushes and pulls.

Take Care of Your Body

Keep your body clean.

Brush and floss your teeth.

Take care of your hair and nails.

Sit and stand up tall.

Wash your hands before and after you eat.

Germs are on things you touch.
Germs can make you sick.

Wash your hands often.

Eat Healthful Foods

Healthful foods give your body energy. You use energy to walk, play, and move. You need energy to help you grow and stay healthy.

Choose healthful foods.

Milk helps your teeth and bones grow.

Fruits and vegetables give you energy.
Bread and cereal do, too.

Meat helps your muscles grow.

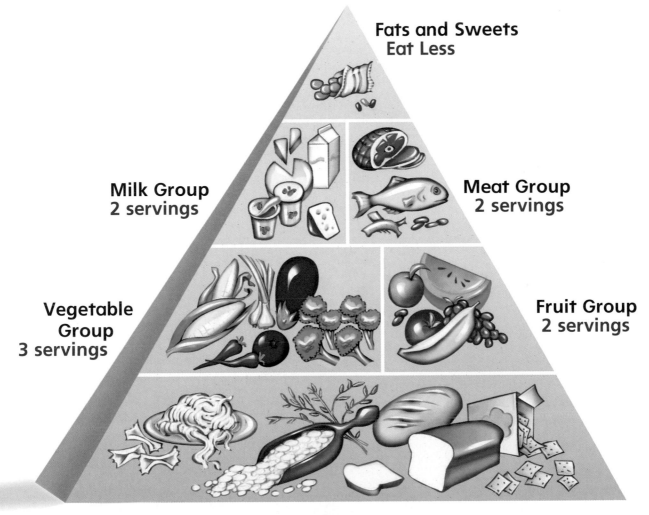

Fats and Sweets
Eat Less

Milk Group
2 servings

Meat Group
2 servings

Vegetable
Group
3 servings

Fruit Group
2 servings

Grain Group
6 servings

Be Active and Rest

Be active every day.
When you are active,
your heart beats faster.
This keeps you healthy
and strong.

Get plenty of
sleep at night.

These things
help you grow!

Stay Healthy

Your body grows and changes.

Get checkups every year.

Doctors and dentists can help you stay healthy as you grow. They can help you get better when you are sick.

Be Safe Indoors

Some things are dangerous. Don't touch them!
Tell an adult when you find something dangerous.

Be Safe Outdoors

Getting Along

Work and play well with others.

Respect one another's feelings.

Show others that you care.

Exploring
Indiana

Your World and You

Now you know that you are a scientist. And your friends are too.

You can do science outside the classroom.

You can do science in backyards and ballparks. In fields and forests. In cities and in the country.

There are things to observe. There are things to count and things to measure. There are sounds to hear.

Where can you begin?

Start with the one thing you know most about. You!

Measure your height. Weigh yourself. Make a list of the sizes of your shoes and clothing.

Add to this list over time. It tells how you change.

Did You Ever Wonder?

Scientists wonder all the time. They wonder about the wonderful. You can too.

Questions help you do science. Ask questions about the world around you.

Did you wonder?

- Why do some plants face the Sun?
- How do insects change during their life?
- Why do some insects stay in Indiana in the winter?
- Why do other insects fly away?
- Where do these insects go?
- How do they find their way back? Find the answers.

How to Begin

Start in a library. Books can help you find answers. If you can not find the answer, you can do an experiment.

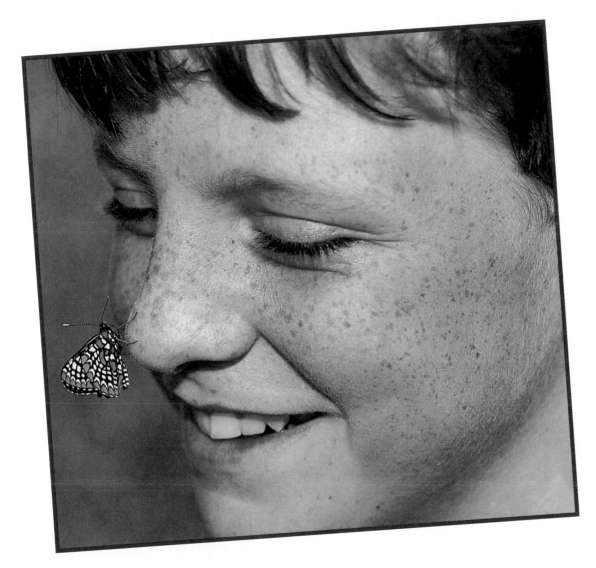

Write what you find out. Draw pictures of your observations.

Share what you discover with others. This is what scientists do, and so can you.

Glossary

The following words are used in the *Exploring Indiana* section that begins each unit. Learn what these words mean. It will help you understand your science readings.

B bat the only mammal that is able to fly, many bats in Indiana sleep through cold winters *(page IN D3)* **Many kinds of bats are helpful because they eat many insects.**

C compass a tool that uses a magnet that points north, is used to help a person move in the right direction *(page IN F5)* **Molly's compass helped us find our way out of the dark woods.**

F forest a large area with many trees, the home for many kinds of animals and plants *(page IN B2)* **The forest was cool and dark. You could hear many animal noises.**

K kernel a seed from the corn plant *(page IN A3)* **If you plant corn kernels, they may grow into a new corn plant.**

L lamprey a fish that uses a sucker-disk to attach itself to another fish *(page IN B5)* **The lamprey attached itself to the side of the trout.**

light a form of energy that we can use to see *(page IN E4)* **I read my science book by the light from an electric lamp.**

M machine a tool used to make work easier *(page IN F2)* **We used a machine to make the wooden boards smooth.**

moon a ball of rock that moves around the Earth once about every twenty-seven days *(page IN D4)* **The Moon appeared large and low in the night sky.**

O opossum an animal that lives in trees in the forest *(page IN B2)* **Opossums are active at night.**

R reflect to bounce back light, heat, or sound *(page IN D4)* **Light can reflect off of glass.**

S sand dunes piles of windblown sand that are often found at the edge of a body of water *(page IN C4)* **Sand dunes are shaped by blowing winds.**

seed the part of a plant that can grow into a new plant *(page IN A2)* **A tomato seed can grow into a new tomato plant.**

W water mill a building that uses the power of moving water to do work, mills often grind grain into flour *(page IN E2)* **The old water mill grinds corn into meal that is used to make cakes.**

white-tailed deer a mammal in the deer family that is becoming more common in many areas *(page IN A5)* **The white-tailed deer in our backyard ate all of Frank's flowers.**

Glossary

A

amphibians animals that start their lives in the water *(page A35)* **Frogs and toads are amphibians.**

Arctic a very cold place near the North Pole *(page B24)* **In the Arctic, snow is on the ground for much of the year.**

attract to pull *(page F38)* **A magnet can attract some metals.**

axis a line through the center of a spinning object *(page D6)* **Earth's axis is an imaginary line that goes from the North Pole to the South Pole.**

axis

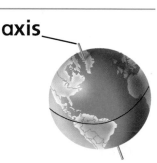

C

chemical change when matter changes into different matter *(page E22)* **When metal rusts, a chemical change happens.**

classify to put things into groups to show how they are alike *(page A4)* **You can classify animals by their legs.**

legs

no legs

LOG ON Visit **www.science.mmhschool.com** to find out more about these words.

communicate to share your ideas with others *(page A36)* **Scientists communicate to learn and to show what they know.**

compare to tell how things are alike and different *(page D10)* **You can compare how the balls are alike and different. One is blue, and the other is red.**

compass a tool with a magnetic needle that always points to Earth's North Pole *(page F49)* **With a compass, you can figure out which direction you are facing.**

condense to change from a gas to a liquid *(page C7)* **Cool air makes water vapor condense.**

constellation a star pattern that makes a picture *(page D40)* **The Big Dipper and the Little Dipper are constellations.**

craters large holes on the surface of the Moon *(page D27)* **Many Moon craters were made by rocks falling from space.**

D

desert a dry habitat that gets very little rainfall *(page B20)* **A desert gets less than ten inches of rain each year.**

draw a conclusion to use what you observe to explain what happens (*page B18*) **You can draw a conclusion about what kind of weather is shown here.**

E

earthquake a shaking of the ground caused by a shift of Earth's crust (*page C20*) **An earthquake causes Earth to change.**

endangered in danger of becoming extinct (*page C48*) **The giant panda is an endangered animal.**

energy what makes matter move or change (*page E32*) **Fireworks give off energy.**

equator the imaginary line around the middle of Earth that separates the northern part from the southern part (*page D16*) **The United States is north of the equator.**

equator

erosion when worn down rocks are carried away (*page C14*) **Erosion caused the Grand Canyon to form.**

evaporate to change from a liquid to a gas *(page C6)* **The boy's sweatshirt dries because the water evaporates.**

extinct when a living thing dies out and no more of its kind are living anywhere on Earth *(page C46)* **The woolly mammoth is extinct.**

F

flower the part of a plant that makes seeds *(page A12)* **Seeds grow inside the flower.**

food chain the order in which energy moves from one living thing to another *(page A41)* **In a food chain, each animal uses another living thing as food.**

food web a group of several food chains that are connected *(page B42)* **Plankton is an important part of the ocean food web.**

force a push or a pull that makes something move or change direction *(page F6)* **The girl moves forward with the help of a force.**

fossils what is left of living things from the past *(page C32)* **Some fossils are animal footprints.**

friction a force that slows down moving things *(page F12)* **A skater stops by using friction.**

fruit the part of a plant that grows around seeds *(page A13)* **The fruit protects the seeds.**

fuel something that gives off heat when it burns *(page E34)* **Wood, natural gas, and oil are fuels.**

fulcrum the fixed point on which a lever rests *(page F21)* **A seesaw rests on a fulcrum.**

G

gas a state of matter that spreads out to fill its container *(page E16)* **A balloon is filled with gas.**

gravity a force that pulls things toward Earth *(page F7)* **Gravity pulls the sled down the hill.**

H

habitat a place where plants and animals can meet their needs *(page B6)* **This goat lives in a mountain habitat.**

heat a kind of energy that can change matter's state *(page E32)* **Heat can change a solid to a liquid.**

I

infer to use what you know to figure something out *(page A14)* **You can infer what kind of animal made these footprints.**

investigate to make a plan and try it out *(page E18)* **You can investigate how to make a magnet attract a paper clip through water.**

L

landslide a sudden movement of soil down a hill *(page C21)* **A landslide can destroy homes.**

larva the stage in the life cycle of a butterfly when the insect is a caterpillar *(page A48)* **A caterpillar is a larva.**

lever a simple machine made of a bar that rests on a fixed point *(page F21)* **You can make a lever with two pencils.**

life cycle shows how a living thing grows, lives, and dies *(page A18)* **A bear's life cycle shows how a bear grows.**

light a kind of energy that lets us see *(page E38)* **We use light from lamps to help us see indoors.**

liquid a state of matter that takes the shape of its container *(page E14)* **Juice is a liquid.**

M

magnetic field the area around a magnet where its force pulls *(page F42)* **A magnetic field can pull through solids, liquids, and gases.**

make a model to make something to show a place or thing *(page B8)* **You can make a model to show where leaf bats live.**

mammals animals with hair or fur that breathe with body parts called lungs *(page A34)* **Female mammals make milk for their babies.**

mass the amount of matter in an object *(page E7)* **A feather has less mass than a crayon.**

matter anything that takes up space and has mass *(page E6)* **Everything in this fish tank is made of matter.**

measure to find out how long, how much, or how warm something is *(page F4)* **You can use a ruler to measure items.**

migrate to move to another place *(page B13)* **In winter these animals migrate to a warmer habitat.**

minerals parts of rock and soil that plants and animals need *(page A7)* **A tree uses minerals in the soil to stay healthy.**

Moon a ball of rock that orbits around Earth *(page D26)* **It takes the Moon about 27 days to finish its orbit around Earth.**

observe to use your senses to learn about the world around you *(page B38)* **Scientists observe things to learn more about them.**

ocean a large, deep body of salt water (*page B40*) **Dolphins live in the ocean.**

orbit the path something takes as it moves around an object (*page D12*) **The Moon moves around Earth in an orbit.**

order to show what happens first, second, third, and last (*page A44*) **When you put things in order you can tell what will happen next.**

oxygen a gas found in the air we breathe (*page A23*) **A whale needs to breathe oxygen to live.**

paleontologist a scientist who studies things that lived long ago (*page C38*) **A paleontologist finds and studies fossils.**

phase the Moon's shape that we can see from Earth (*page D32*) **We see phases of the Moon because we see different parts of its lit side.**

physical change to change the size or shape of matter (*page E20*) **When you cut food, a physical change happens.**

pitch how high or how low a sound is
(page E47) **You can play a high pitch or a low pitch on a xylophone.**

planet a huge object that travels around the Sun *(page D44)* **Saturn is a planet in our solar system.**

poles the ends of a magnet where the pull is strongest *(page F40)* **Every magnet has two poles.**

pollen the powder inside a flower that can make seeds grow *(page A16)* **The bee carries the pollen from flower to flower.**

pollution the effect of harmful things in water, air, or land *(page B46)* **Pollution hurts living things.**

pond a fresh water habitat in which the water stays in one place *(page B34)* **Beavers build their homes in a pond.**

precipitation water falling from the sky as rain, snow, and hail *(page C9)* **Rain is a kind of precipitation.**

predator an animal that hunts another animal for food *(page A40)* **Sharks are predators.**

predict to use what you know to tell what you think will happen *(page A10)* **You can predict what might grow from these seeds.**

prey an animal that is hunted *(page A40)* **The bird is the cat's prey.**

property something that tells you about an object *(page E8)* **Big, brown, and fuzzy are all properties of this bear.**

pupa the stage in the life cycle of a butterfly when a caterpillar makes a hard case around itself *(page A48)* **Inside the hard case, the pupa changes into a butterfly.**

R

rain forest a habitat where it rains almost every day *(page B16)* **A rain forest can get more than 70 inches of rain each year.**

ramp a simple machine with a slanted surface *(page F26)* **A ramp makes it easier to move from place to place.**

recycle to use waste to make new things that can be used again *(page B49)* **We can recycle paper, glass, cans, and plastic.**

reflect to bounce off an object *(page E38)* **A mirror reflects light.**

refraction when light bends as it passes through something *(page E39)* **Refraction can make something look bigger.**

repel to push away from *(page F41)* **The poles of these magnets repel each other.**

reptiles animals with scaly skin *(page A34)* **Snakes are reptiles.**

rotate to spin *(page D6)* **Earth rotates on its axis.**

rotates —

S

seeds the plant parts that can grow into new plants *(page A13)* **Seeds begin to grow when they get water, warmth, and air.**

shelter a place where an animal can live and be safe *(page A42)* **Foxes find shelter in a hole.**

simple machine something that helps you lift or move an object *(page F20)* **A ramp is a simple machine.**

skeleton a full set of bones *(page C39)*
A dinosaur skeleton helps scientists learn what dinosaurs looked like.

solar system the Sun, nine planets, and all of their moons *(page D44)* **The Sun is the center of our solar system.**

solid a state of matter that has a shape of its own *(page E12)* **This wooden block is a solid.**

sound a kind of energy that you hear *(page E44)* **When you crash cymbals together, they make a loud sound.**

star a hot ball in the sky that makes its own light *(page D38)* **A star looks tiny because it is so far away from Earth.**

stream a fresh water habitat with moving water *(page B36)* **Plants and animals live in and around a stream.**

Sun the closest star to Earth *(page D7)* **The Sun gives Earth heat and light.**

T

temperature how warm something is
(page E9) **You can measure temperature
by using a thermometer.**

V

vibrate to move back and forth *(page E44)*
**When a string vibrates, you can hear
sound.**

volcano a mountain formed when hot,
melted rock builds up and bursts through
the surface of Earth *(page C22)* **Mt. St. Helens
is a volcano that erupted in 1980.**

volume the amount of space that a thing
takes up *(page E15)* **You can measure the
volume of a liquid with measuring cups.**

W

water cycle the movement of water
between the ground and sky *(page C8)* **Rain
and snow are parts of the water cycle.**

water vapor water that has become a gas
(page C6) **When water boils, some of the
water turns into water vapor.**

woodland forest a habitat that gets
enough rain and sunlight for trees to
grow well *(page B10)* **Many plants and
animals live in a woodland forest.**

Credits

Cover Photos: c. Joe McDonald/McDonald Wildlife Photography; bkgd. Daryl Benson/Masterfile; spine Joe McDonald/McDonald Wildlife Photography; Back Cover: bkgd. Daryl Benson/Masterfile; t.l. Frank Fournier/Contact Press Images; t.r. Tim Parsley/Index Stock Imagery; c.l. John Lamb/Stone/Getty Images; c.r. Frank Zullo/Photo Researchers, Inc.; b.l. Donovan Reese/Stone/Getty Images; b.r. Karl Weatherly/Stone/Getty Images. Endpaper: Daryl Benson/Masterfile

Photography Credits: All photos are by Macmillan/McGraw-Hill (MMH) and Dave Mager for MMH, Ray Boudreau for MMH, Michael Groen for MMH, Ken Karp for MMH, Ron Tanaka for MMH, and David Waitz for MMH except as noted below:

i: bkgd. Daryl Benson/Masterfile; t.l. Zefa Visual Media-Germany/Index Stock Imagery; b.l. D. Cox/OSF/Animals Animals. iii: Robert Franz/Index Stock Imagery. iv: bkgd. Taxi/Getty Images; t. NASA/CORBIS; c., b. Courtesy, Sally Ride. v: l. Siede Preis/PhotoDisc/Getty Images; r. Jeff L. Lepore/Photo Researchers, Inc. vi: l. Keren Su/Stock Boston; b. Paul Zahl/Photo Researchers, Inc. vii: l. Tim Parsley/Index Stock Imagery; r. Leonard Lee Rue/Stock Boston. viii: l. John Lamb/Stone/Getty Images; b. Bob Burch/Bruce Coleman, Inc. ix: l. Frank Zullo/Photo Researchers Inc; b. NASA/Science Force/Photo Researchers, Inc. x: l. Donovan Reese/Stone/Getty Images; b. Bill Gallery/Stock Boston. xi: l. Karl Weatherly/Stone/Getty Images; b. Will Ryan/The Stock Market/CORBIS. xv: t.l., t.r. PhotoDisc/Getty Images. xvi: t.c., c., c.l. PhotoDisc/Getty Images; b.l. Siede Preis/PhotoDisc/Getty Images. SO: Susan Rosenthal/CORBIS. S0-S1: Michael & Patricia Fogden/CORBIS. S2: David Young-Wolff/PhotoEdit. S3: Jeff L. Lepore/Photo Researchers, Inc. S4-S5: F. Sieb/Robertstock.com. S6: C Squared Studios/PhotoDisc/Getty Images; S7: Siede Preis/PhotoDisc/Getty Images. S8-S9: Burke/Triolo Productions/Brand X Pictures. S10-S11: Marc Romanelli/Getty Images. S12: David Young-Wolff/PhotoEdit. S13: bkgd. Artbase Inc.; l. Michael Ederegger/DRK Photo; t.r. D. Suzio/Photo Researchers, Inc.; c.r. Gary Moszaros/Photo Researchers, Inc.; b.r. Burke/Triolo Productions/Brand X Pictures. S14-S15: Royalty-Free/CORBIS/MAGMA. S16: l. David H. Wells/CORBIS. AO: Frank Fournier/Contact Press Images. A0-A1: Keren Su/Stock Boston. A1: Frank Fournier/Contact Press Images. A2-A3: John Gerlach/DRK Photo. A4-A5: Jeanne White/Photo Researchers, Inc. A6: l. Tom Bean/DRK Photo; l. inset Aaron Haupt/Stock Boston; r. inset E.R. Degginger/Color-Pic, Inc. A6-A7: sky John Eastcott/DRK Photo; soil Susanna Price/DK Images; c. E.R. Degginger/Color-Pic, Inc. A7: l. Siede Preis/PhotoDisc/PictureQuest; r. Ross Durant/FoodPix. A8: Christian Grzimek/Photo Researchers, Inc. A8-A9: HOLT Studios/Photo Researchers, Inc. A9: r. Patti Murray/Earth Scenes; l. Alan & Linda Detrick/Photo Researchers, Inc. A10-A11: John Kaprielian/Photo Researchers, Inc. A12: flowers and plant Leslye Borden/PhotoEdit; tomatoes Mary Kate Denny/PhotoEdit. A12-A13: soil Susanna Price/DK Images. A13: l. Johnny's Selected Seeds; r. David/Jules Murray/Selmes/DK Images. A14-A15: Richard Hutchings/PhotoEdit. A15: t.r. PhotoDisc/Getty Images; t.c.r. Spencer Grant/PhotoEdit. A16: l. Patti Murray/Earth Scenes; r. Patricia Agre/Photo Researchers, Inc.; bee M.P.L. Fogden/Bruce Coleman, Inc. A17: t. Michael Newman/PhotoEdit; b.l. Jerry Howard/Stock Boston; r. Felicia Martinez/PhotoEdit. A18: b.l. Leonard Lessin/Peter Arnold, Inc.; b.c. Alfred B. Thomas/Earth Scenes; roots Dwight Kuhn Photography. A18-A19: t. John Kaprielian/Photo Researchers, Inc.; b. Susanna Price/DK Images. A19: Patti Murray/Earth Scenes. A20-A21: Tom Salyer/Silver Image for MMH. A22: t.l. David Young-Wolff/PhotoEdit; inset Aaron Haupt/Stock Boston; b.l. RDF/Visuals Unlimited; b.r. Alan & Linda Detrick/Photo Researchers, Inc. A22-A23: Richard Shiell/Earth Scenes. A23: t.l. Russell Lincoln/Stock Boston; t.r. Myrleen Cate/PhotoEdit; b.l. RDF/Visuals Unlimited. A24: l. Maximillian Stock Ltd./Earth Scenes. A26: C.C. Lockwood/Bruce Coleman Inc. A30-A31: Douglas Faulkner/Photo Researchers, Inc. A32: t. Donald Specker/Animals Animals; b. John Cancalosi/Stock Boston. A32-A33: bkgd. Tom Brakefield/DRK Photo. A33: t.l. Jim Brandenburg/Minden Pictures; b.l. Tim Rock/Animals Animals; c.l. Frans Lanting/Minden Pictures; c.r. Konrad Wothe/Minden Pictures; t.r. Lisa Husar/DRK Photo; b.r. Allen Blake Sheldon/Animals Animals. A34: t. Breck Kent/Animals Animals; c. Wayne Lynch/DRK Photo; b. Anup Shah/DRK Photo. A35: t. Russell C. Hansen/Peter Arnold, Inc.; c. Paul Zahl/Photo Researchers, Inc.; b. Patrice Ceisel/Stock Boston. A36-A37: Rafi Bewn-Shahar/DRK Photo. A38-A39: Carl Sams/Peter Arnold, Inc. A39: r. Johnny Johnson/DRK Photo; b. Mitsuaki Iwago/Minden Pictures. A40: t. James Watt/Animals Animals; b.l. Laura Riley/Bruce Coleman, Inc.; b.r. John Gerlach/DRK Photo. A41: t.r. John Kaprielian/Photo Researchers, Inc.; inset D. Cavagnaro/Peter Arnold, Inc.; l. Walter E. Harvay/Photo Researchers, Inc.; b. Jane Burton/Bruce Coleman, Inc. A42: b. Paul Berquist/Animals Animals. A42-A43: Frans Lanting/Minden Pictures. A43: l. C. Allan Morgan/Peter Arnold, Inc.; r. Olen S. Hansen/Photo Researchers, Inc. A44-A45: Margot Conte/Animals Animals. A46: Wayne Lynch/DRK Photo. A46-A47: Lisa & Mike Husar/DRK Photo. A47: t. Stephen J. Krasemann/DRK Photo; b. Tom & Pat Leeson/DRK Photo. A48: Kim Taylor/DK Images. A48-A49: John Eastcott/DRK Photo. A49: Kim Taylor/DK Images. A51: t. Rod Planck/Photo Researchers, Inc.; c. Norbert Wu/Minden Pictures; b. D. Cavagnaro/DRK Photo. A53: t. Anup Shah/DRK Photo; b. Kim Taylor/DK Images. A54-A55: Dan Helms/National Geographic Image Collection. A56: b. Jane Burton/Bruce Coleman, Inc. BO: Tim Parsley/Index Stock Imagery. B0-B1: bkgd. Reinhard Eisele/CORBIS; inset PhotoDisc/Getty Images. B2-B3: Claudia Adams/Dembinsky Photo Associates. B4-B5: Tom Walker/Stock Boston. B5: b. Lynda Richardson/CORBIS. B6: l. George Bernard/Animals Animals; r. M.C. Chamberlain/DRK Photo. B6-B7: William Johnson/Stock Boston. B7: t. Fritz Polking/Dembinsky Photo Associates; b. E.R. Degginger/Dembinsky Photo Associates. B8-B9: David Ulmer/Stock Boston. B10: l. DPA/Dembinsky Photo Associates; r. Robert Ginn/PhotoEdit. B10-B11: Owen Franken/Stock Boston. B11: l. Clouds Hill Imaging Ltd./CORBIS; b. Joe McDonald/Animals Animals; r. Tom & Pat Leeson/DRK Photo. B12: t. Terry Donnelly/Dembinsky Photo Associates; c. Skip Moody/Dembinsky Photo Associates; b.l. DPA/Dembinsky Photo Associates; b.r. Anthony Mercieca/Dembinsky Photo Associates. B13: t. Barbara Gerlach/Dembinsky Photo Associates; t.c. Mark Newman/Bruce Coleman, Inc.; b.c. Breck P. Kent/Animals Animals; b. Adam Jones/Dembinsky Photo Associates. B14: Michael Fogden/DRK Photo. B14-B15: Thomas Fletcher/Stock Boston. B16: Kevin & Suzette Hanley/Animals Animals. B16-B17: Tom & Pat Leeson/DRK Photo. B17: l. Richard La Val/Animals Animals; r. G.W. Willis/Animals Animals. B18-B19: Adam Jones/Dembinsky Photo Associates. B20: l. Jon Gerlach/DRK Photo; b. E.R. Degginger/Dembinsky Photo Associates. B20-B21: Joe McDonald/Earth Scenes. B21: C. Allan Morgan/DRK Photo. B22: Johnny Johnson/DRK Photo. B22-B23: Tom Walker/Stock Boston. B24: l. Eastcott/Momatiuk/Earth Scenes; b. Matthew Neil McVay/Stock Boston. B24-B25: Leonard Lee Rue III/Animals Animals. B25: t. Phyllis Greenberg/Animals Animals; b. Mark J. Thomas/Dembinsky Photo Associates. B26: t.l. Terry Donnelly/Dembinsky Photo Associates; t.r. Joe McDonald/Earth Scenes; c. Hans Strand/Stone/Getty Images; b. Thomas Fletcher/Stock Boston. B29: t.l. E.R. Degginger/Dembinsky Photo Associates; t.c. David Ulmer/Stock Boston; t.r. C. Allan Morgan/DRK Photo; b.r. Tom Walker/Stock Boston. B30-B31: bkgd. Pat & Tom Leeson/Photo Researchers, Inc. B32-B33: S. Nielsen/DRK Photo. B34: t. George Godfrey/Earth Scenes; b. Jim Battles/Dembinsky Photo Associates. B34-B35: Joe McDonald/Animals Animals. B35: t.l. Rod Planck/Dembinsky Photo Associates; t.r. Johnny Johnson/Animals Animals; b. John Mitchell/Photo Researchers, Inc. B36: t. K. Ringland/Animals Animals; b. Jim Roetzel/Dembinsky Photo Associates. B36-B37: Willard Clay/Dembinsky Photo Associates. B37: l. Hans Reinhard/Bruce Coleman, Inc.; r. Leonard Lee Rue/Stock Boston. B38-B39: Jeff Foott/DRK Photo. B40: l. Susan Blanchet/Dembinsky Photo Associates; r. Reinhard Dirscherl/Alamy. B40-B41: bkgd. Villoch-V&W/Bruce Coleman, Inc.; t. Doug Perrine/DRK Photo. B41: t. Chuck Place/Stock Boston; b.l. D.P. Wilson/Dembinsky Photo Associates; b.r. P. Parks/Animals Animals. B42: b.l. E.R. Degginger/Earth Scenes; b.r. Norbert Wu/DRK Photo; c. P. Parks/Animals Animals. B42-B43: bkgd. John Gerlach/Earth Scenes; t. Kim Heacox/DRK Photo; b. Jack Grove/PhotoEdit. B43: Jeffry Myers/Stock Boston. B44-B45: M. Harvey/DRK Photo. B46: t. Thomas R. Fletcher/Stock Boston; b. M. Harvey/DRK Photo. B47: t. A. Ramey/Stock Boston; b. Michael Newman/PhotoEdit. B48: t. Lawrence Migdale/Stock Boston; b. Donald Dietz/Stock Boston. B49: t. Zig Leszczynski/Earth Scenes; b. Julie Houck/Stock Boston. B51: t. Group III Kerr/Bruce Coleman, Inc. B53: t.l. George H.H. Huey/Animals Animals; t.r., c.l. Jim Battles/Dembinsky Photo Associates; c.r. Jeffry Myers/Stock Boston. B54: American Museum of Natural History. B54-B55: c. Denis Finnin/American Museum of Natural History; bkgd. Villoch-V&W/Bruce Coleman, Inc. CO: John Lamb/Stone/Getty Images. C0-C1: James Randklev/Stone/Getty Images. C2-C3: Larry Miller/Photo Researchers, Inc. C4-C5: David Young-Wolff/PhotoEdit. C6: Jon Serafin for MMH. C7: l. Jon Serafin for MMH; r. Scott Smith/Animals Animals. C10: t. Adam Jones/Dembinsky Photo Associates; b. Don Smetzer/PhotoEdit. C10-C11: D. Lloyd/Weatherstock. C11: Warren Faidley/Weatherstock. C12-C13: David A. Bast/Photo Researchers, Inc. C14-C15: Dick Canby/DRK Photo. C15: t. Bob Burch/Bruce Coleman, Inc.; b. Terry Donnelly/Dembinsky Photo Associates. C16-C17: t. Tom Bean/DRK Photo; b. M.H. Black/Bruce Coleman, Inc. C17: David Woodfall/DRK Photo. C18-C19: Tom McHugh/Photo Researchers, Inc. C20: Norman O. Tomalin/Bruce Coleman, Inc. C20-C21: Tom McHugh/Photo Researchers, Inc. C22: Pat & Tom Leeson/Photo Researchers, Inc. C22-C23: David Weintraub/Photo Researchers, Inc. C23: t. David Weintraub/Photo Researchers, Inc.; b. Michael P. Gadomski/Earth Scenes. C24: t.l. Comstock Images/Alamy. C27: t.l. Don Smetzer/PhotoEdit; t.r. Adam Jones/Dembinsky Photo Associates; b.r. Terry Donnelly/Dembinsky Photo Associates. C28-C29: Sinclair Stammers/Photo Researchers, Inc. C30-C31: T.A. Wiewandt/DRK Photo. C32: t. Francois Gohier/Photo Researchers, Inc.; l. Joy Spurr/Bruce Coleman, Inc.; b. Dr. David R. Schwimmer/Bruce Coleman, Inc. C32-C33: J.C. Carton/Bruce Coleman, Inc. C33: t. Sinclair Stammers/Photo Researchers, Inc.; b. Tom McHugh & Natural History Museum of L.A. County/Photo Researchers, Inc. C35: David Schwimmer/Bruce Coleman, Inc. C36-C37: Bob Burch/Bruce Coleman, Inc. C38: Pete Larson/Black Hills Institute. C38-C39: Ira Block/National Geographic Image Collection. C39: Ira Block/National Geographic Image Collection. C40: t. Bob Burch/Bruce Coleman, Inc.; b. Michael Fogden/Animals Animals. C41: t.l. Claudia Adams/Dembinsky Photo Associates; t.r. Stephen J. Krasemann/DRK Photo; b.l. Francois Gohier/Photo Researchers, Inc.; b.r. Stan Osolinski/Dembinsky Photo Associates. C44-C45: Tom & Pat Leeson/DRK Photo. C46: t. Don & Pat Valenti/DRK Photo; b. Stephen J. Krasemann/DRK Photo. C46-C47: Francois Gohier/Photo Researchers, Inc. C47: t. George Bernard/Animals Animals; b. Michael Fogden/Bruce Coleman, Inc. C48: t. Maresa Pryor/Earth Scenes; t.c. Henry Ausloos/Animals Animals; b.c. Alan D. Carey/Photo Researchers, Inc.; b.l. Pat & Rae Hagan/Bruce Coleman, Inc. C48-C49: David N. Davis/Photo Researchers, Inc. C49: t. Erwin & Peggy Bauer/Bruce Coleman, Inc.; b. Bruce M. Herman/Photo Researchers, Inc. C52: t. Bob Burch/Bruce Coleman, Inc.; b. Michael Fogden/Animals Animals. C53: t. Francois Gohier/Photo Researchers, Inc. C54: O. Louis Mazzatenta/National Geographic Image Collection. C54-C55: O. Louis Mazzatenta/National Geographic Image Collection. C55: CORBIS. DO: Frank Zullo/Photo Researchers, Inc. D0-D1: Science Photo Library/Photo Researchers, Inc. D2-D3: NASA. D4: Rafael Macia/Photo Researchers, Inc. D4-D5: Rafael Macia/Photo Researchers, Inc. D6: Jonathan Nourok/PhotoEdit. D6-D7: Byron Jorjorian/Bruce Coleman, Inc. D7: Jisas/Lockheed/Science Photo Library/Photo Researchers, Inc. D10: Don & Pat Valenti/DRK Photo. D10-D11: Robert Aschenbrenner/Stock Boston. D14-D15: Dennis Flaherty/Photo Researchers, Inc. D16: t. James Blank/Bruce Coleman, Inc.; b. Antipodes/Gamma Sport. D17: Jacques Jangoux/Photo Researchers, Inc. D20: Jacques Jangoux/Photo Researchers, Inc. D22-D23: BMDO/NRL/LLNL/Science Photo Library/Photo Researchers, Inc. D24: t. David Nunuk/Photo Researchers, Inc.; b. Bruce Coleman, Inc. D24-D25: John W. Bova/Photo Researchers, Inc. D26-D27: David Nunuk/Photo Researchers, Inc. D28: moon David Nunuk/Photo Researchers, Inc. D28-D29: t. Images Colour Library/Natural Selection; b. Novastock/Photo Researchers, Inc. D29: t. David Nunuk/Photo Researchers, Inc. D30: John Sanford/Science Photo Library/Photo Researchers, Inc. D30-D31: Larry Landolfi/Photo Researchers, Inc. D32: John Sanford/Science Photo Library/Photo Researchers, Inc. D33: l. John W. Bova/Photo Researchers, Inc.; c., r. John Sanford/Science Photo Library/Photo Researchers, Inc. D34: l., c. John Sanford/Science Photo Library/Photo Researchers, Inc.; r. John Bova/Photo Researchers, Inc. D35: John Sanford/Science Photo Library/Photo Researchers, Inc. D36-D37: John Foster/Photo Researchers, Inc. D38: inset David Parker/Photo Researchers, Inc.; b.l. Dr. E.I. Robson/Photo Researchers, Inc. D38-D39: Allan

Morton/Dennis Milon/Science Photo Library/Photo Researchers, Inc. D39: Celestial Image Picture Co./Science Photo Library/Photo Researchers, Inc. D40-D41: t. Pekka Parviainen/Science Photo Library/Photo Researchers, Inc.; b. John W. Bova/Photo Researchers, Inc. D41: Jerry Schad/Photo Researchers, Inc. D42-D43: CORBIS. D46: t.l. U.S. Geological Survey/Photo Researchers, Inc.; t.c. NASA/Science Photo Library/Photo Researchers, Inc.; b. Science Source/Photo Researchers, Inc.; b.c. NASA. D46-D47: t. NASA/Science Force/Photo Researchers, Inc.; b. NASA/Bruce Coleman, Inc. D47: t. ASP/Science Source/Photo Researchers, Inc.; c. StockTrek/PhotoDisc/Getty Images; b. NASA/Science Photo Library/Photo Researchers, Inc. D48: l. NASA/Science Source/Photo Researchers, Inc.; r. Space Telescope Science Institute/NASA/Science Photo Library/Photo Researchers, Inc. D48-D49: NASA/Science Photo Library/Photo Researchers, Inc. D49: t. NASA/Science Photo Library/Photo Researchers, Inc.; b. Julian Baum/Science Photo Library/Photo Researchers, Inc. D53: l. John Sanford/Science Photo Library/Photo Researchers, Inc.; r. John W. Bova/Photo Researchers, Inc. D54: NASA. D54-D55: NASA/Roger Ressmeyer/CORBIS. D56: t. Dennis Flaherty/Photo Researchers, Inc. EO: Donovan Reese/Stone/Getty Images. E0-E1: J.A. Kraulis/Masterfile. E2-E3: Darrell Wong/Stone/Getty Images. E4-E5: Joe Viesti/Viesti Associates, Inc E8-E9: John Serafin for MMH. E10-E11: Tony Freeman/PhotoEdit. E16-E17: t. Bill Gallery/Stock Boston; b. Jose L. Pelaez/The Stock Market/CORBIS. E22: t. Walter Hodges/Stone/Getty Images; c. David Langley/The Stock Market/CORBIS. E26: b.r. David Langley/The Stock Market/CORBIS. E27: t.l. Jose L. Pelaez/The Stock Market/CORBIS. E28-E29: Bob Gomel/The Stock Market/CORBIS. E30-E31: Tom Salyer/Silver Image for MMH. E34: Eyewire. E34-E35: Robert Brenner/PhotoEdit. E35: t. Ronnie Kaufman/The Stock Market/CORBIS. E36-E37: Greg Meadors/Stock Boston. E38: Tony Freeman/PhotoEdit. E38-E39: Sanford/Agliolo/The Stock Market/CORBIS. E39: t. David Frazier/David R. Frazier Photolibrary; b. Michael Newman/PhotoEdit. E40: Sakura/Black Sheep/Natural Selection Stock Photography. E40-E41: Peter Beck/The Stock Market/CORBIS. E41: t. The Stock Market/CORBIS; b. Bob Thomason/Stone/Getty Images. E42-E43: Keren Su/China Span/Alamy. E44-E45: SuperStock. E46: t. DiMaggio/Kalish/The Stock Market/CORBIS; b. SuperStock. E47: t. Chris Collins/The Stock Market/CORBIS; b.l. David Allan Brandt/Stone/Getty Images. E48-E49: Norbert Wu. E50: r. Bettmann/CORBIS. E53: t.l. The Stock Market/CORBIS; b.c. Michael Newman/PhotoEdit; b.r. Tony Freeman/PhotoEdit. E54-E55: Herral Long. FO: Karl Weatherly/Stone/Getty Images. F0-F1: Richard Price/Taxi/Getty Images. F2-F3: SuperStock. F6 : SuperStock. F6-F7: Gabe Palmer/The Stock Market/CORBIS. F7: Tom Rosenthal/SuperStock. F8: t. Cosmo Condina/Stone/Getty Images; b. SuperStock. F9: l. C Squared Studios/PhotoDisc/Getty Images; r. Joe Prater/Visuals Unlimited, Inc. F10-F11: William R. Sallaz/Duomo. F13: l. Lori Adamski Peek/Stone/Getty Images; r. Michael Dwyer/Stock Boston. F14: Tom Salyer/Silver Image for MMH. F16-F17: Mark Cooper/The Stock Market/CORBIS. F17: John Serafin for MMH. F22: t. Lawrence Migdale. F22-F23: Lon C. Diehl/PhotoEdit. F23: Michael Newman/PhotoEdit. F24-F25: Kenneth Garrett/National Geographic Image Collection. F28: l. SuperStock. F28-F29: SuperStock. F29: l. Jeff Greenberg/Visuals Unlimited, Inc.; r. Robert Fried/Stock Boston. F31: Joe Sohm/Chromosohm/Stock Connection/PictureQuest. F32: l. SuperStock; r. Lon C. Diehl/PhotoEdit. F33: t.l. Lawrence Migdale; t.c. Robert Fried/Stock Boston. F34-F35: Vaughn Fleming/Photo Researchers, Inc. F46: t. John Serafin for MMH. F47: David R. Frazier/David R. Frazier Photolibrary. F48: Tom Van Sant/Photo Researchers, Inc. F48-F49: Will Ryan/The Stock Market/CORBIS. F49: Peter Beck/The Stock Market/CORBIS. F54: Courtesy, Fred Jeffers. F54-F55: Royalty-Free/CORBIS. R1: Daryl Benson/Masterfile. R8: b.l., b.r. Dennis Flaherty/Photo Researchers, Inc. R14: PhotoDisc/Getty Images. R15: John Kaprielian/Photo Researchers, Inc. R19: t. Pronk & Associates. R23: l.

PhotoDisc/Getty Images; r. Maximilian Weinzierl/Alamy. R24: l. PhotoDisc/Getty Images; r. Tom Rosenthal/SuperStock. R26: l. Charles D. Winters/Photo Researchers, Inc. R26-R27: Bonnie Sue/Photo Researchers, Inc. R27: Tony Freeman/PhotoEdit. R29: t.r., insets, b.r. PhotoDisc/Getty Images; b.l. G.K. & Vikki Hart/PhotoDisc/Getty Images. R30: PhotoDisc/Getty Images. R31: Roman Sapecki for MMH. R32: t.l. Jim Whitmer/FPG International/Getty Images; t.r. PhotoDisc/Getty Images; b.l., b.r. Roman Sapecki and/or Lew Lause for MMH. R33: David Young-Wolff/PhotoEdit. R34: t. Roman Sapecki and/or Lew Lause for MMH. R36: t.l. Radlund & Associates/Brand X Pictures/PictureQuest; t.r. Lori Adamski Peek/Stone/Getty Images; b.l. Laura Dwight/Peter Arnold, Inc.; b.r. PhotoDisc/Getty Images. R37: t. Adam Smith/Taxi/Getty Images; c. PhotoDisc/Getty Images; b. Ed Wheeler/The Stock Market/CORBIS. R38: b.l. PhotoDisc/Getty Images; b.r. Jerry Schad/Photo Researchers, Inc. R40: PhotoDisc/Getty Images. R41: t. Paul Zahl/Photo Researchers, Inc.; t.c. Tom Walker/Stock Boston; b.c. David Langley/The Stock Market/CORBIS. R42: t. to b. 3. Peter Beck/The Stock Market/CORBIS; 4. Scott Smith/Animals Animals; 5. Jerry Schad/Photo Researchers, Inc.; 6. BMDO/NRL/LLNL/Science Photo Library/Photo Researchers, Inc.; 7. Adam Jones/Dembinsky Photo Associates. R43: t. to b. 1. Warren Faidley/Weatherstock; 2. Norman O. Tomalin/Bruce Coleman, Inc.; 3. Tom & Pat Leeson/DRK Photo; 4. Bob Gomel/The Stock Market/CORBIS; 5. Jonathan Nourok/PhotoEdit; 6. Dick Canby/DRK Photo. R44: t. to b. 1. Jon Serafin for MMH; 2. Francois Gohier/Photo Researchers, Inc.; 3. Patricia Agre/Photo Researchers, Inc.; 4. l. John Kaprielian/Photo Researchers, Inc.; 4. inset D. Cavagnaro/Peter Arnold, Inc.; 4. r. Walter E. Harvay/Photo Researchers, Inc.; 5. l. Norbert Wu/DRK Photo; 5. t. Kim Heacox/DRK Photo; 5. r. Jeffry Myers/Stock Boston; 5. b. Jack Grove/PhotoEdit; 6. Gabe Palmer/The Stock Market/CORBIS. R45: t. to b. 1. Francois Gohier/Photo Researchers, Inc.; 2. Michael Dwyer/Stock Boston; 3. l. Jerry Howard/Stock Boston; 3. r. Tom & Pat Leeson/PhotoEdit; 4. Walter Hodges/Stone/Getty Images; 5. Jose L. Pelaez/The Stock Market/CORBIS; 6. Tom Rosenthal/SuperStock. R46: 1. Tom Walker/Stock Boston; 2. Charles D. Winters/Photo Researchers, Inc.; 3. T.A. Wiewandt/DRK Photo; 5. Tom McHugh/Photo Researchers, Inc.; 6. Kim Taylor/DK Images. R47: t. to b. 2. l. Lisa & Mike Husar/DRK Photo; 2. c. Stephen J. Krasemann/DRK Photo; 2. r. Tom & Pat Leeson/DRK Photo; 3. The Stock Market/CORBIS; 5. Vaughn Fleming/Photo Researchers, Inc.; 7. Mark J. Thomas/Dembinsky Photo Associates. R48: t. to b. 2. John Serafin for MMH; 4. Leonard Lee Rue III/Animals Animals; 6. David Nunuk/Photo Researchers, Inc. R49: 1. Doug Perrine/DRK Photo; 3. Johnny Johnson/DRK Photo; 4. Pete Larson; 5. John Sanford/Science Photo Library/Photo Researchers, Inc. R50: t. to b. 1. Chris Collins/The Stock Market/CORBIS; 2. NASA/Bruce Coleman, Inc.; 4. bkgd. Patti Murray/Earth Scenes; 5. Zig Leszczynski/Earth Scenes; 6. Joe McDonald/Animals Animals; 7. Warren Faidley/Weatherstock; 8. James Watt/Animals Animals. R51: t. to b. 1. l. Leonard Lessin/Peter Arnold, Inc.; 1. r. Jerry Howard/Stock Boston; 2. t. Walter E. Harvay/Photo Researchers, Inc.; 2. b. Jane Burton/Bruce Coleman, Inc.; 3. Stephen J. Krasemann/DRK Photo; 4. Kim Taylor/DK Images; 5. Thomas Fletcher Stock Boston; 6. Robert Fried/Stock Boston; 7. Julie Houck/Stock Boston. R52: t. to b. 1. Tony Freeman/PhotoEdit; 2. Michael Newman/PhotoEdit; 4. Wayne Lynch/DRK Photo; 5. Leonard Lessin/Peter Arnold, Inc.; 6. Tom & Pat Leeson/DRK Photo; 7. Jeff Greenberg/Visuals Unlimited, Inc. R53: t. to b. 1. Bob Burch/Bruce Coleman, Inc.; 4. Celestial Image Picture Co./Science Photo Library/Photo Researchers, Inc.; 5. Willard Clay/Dembinsky Photo Associates; 6. Byron Jorjorian/Bruce Coleman, Inc. R54: t. to b. 2. SuperStock; 3. David Weintraub/Photo Researchers, Inc.; 6. David Ulmer/Stock Boston.